Crocheted Succulents

T0339210

Crocheted Succulents

CACTI & OTHER SUCCULENT PLANTS TO MAKE

EMMA VARNAM

For Lucy and Christine

First published 2019 by
Guild of Master Craftsman Publications Ltd
Castle Place, 166 High Street, Lewes,
East Sussex BN7 1XU, UK

Reprinted 2019, 2021, 2022, 2024

Text © Emma Varnam, 2019
Copyright in the Work © GMC Publications Ltd, 2019

ISBN 978 1 78494 504 6

PUBLISHER: Jonathan Bailey
PRODUCTION: Jim Bulley
SENIOR PROJECT EDITOR: Wendy McAngus
EDITOR: Nicola Hodgson
PATTERN CHECKING: Jude Roust
MANAGING ART EDITOR: Gilda Pacitti
DESIGN & ART DIRECTION: Wayne Blades
PHOTOGRAPHER: Neal Grundy
TECHNIQUE ILLUSTRATIONS: Martin Woodward

Colour origination by GMC Reprographics

Printed and bound in China

Contents

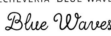

Introduction

Oh, the joy of creating this book for you! I don't know when I have laughed or jumped up and down more with excitement. Each of the projects brings a beaming smile to my face and I hope they do the same for you.

Succulent plants have grown in popularity in recent years, as our climate gets hotter and more of us are able to grow these plants outside in pots. I started growing succulents about two years ago and my son loves to collect cacti too. We have attended courses to learn how to look after our plants and how to propagate them.

Then it occurred to me that it would be fun to create a crocheted version of our collection. The techniques of crochet are perfectly suited to creating these cute specimens, and these versions are immune to the perils of overwatering or drought. They also have very attractive patterns and symmetry, making them a curious delight.

In some of the patterns I have embellished the plant with flowers and pompoms to create an exotic look. I have also created spines and spikes using fashion yarns.

To display them, I mixed the projects up with my living succulent and cacti collection on our bookshelves. It is so difficult to tell them apart that few people visiting my house realized that they have been made simply with a length of yarn and a hook.

So what are you waiting for? Even if you don't have green fingers you can soon be the proud creator of a stunning indoor garden.

Happy crocheting!

Baseball Plant

This is a simple succulent pattern that you can use as a way to practise your amigurumi technique. Here we have displayed the plants in real pots, but if you like you can also crochet pots for extra colour and cuteness.

FINISHED SIZE

The succulent is approximately 2¾in (7cm) in diameter.

TENSION

Tension is not essential for this project.

YOU WILL NEED

- Stylecraft Special DK, 100% acrylic (323yd/295m per 100g ball): 1 ball in 1820 Duck Egg
- 3.5mm (UK9:USE/4) crochet hook
- 1 x ⅜in (10mm) button (optional)
- Polyester stuffing
- Tapestry needle
- Plant pot approximately 2½in (6cm) in diameter
- Cocktail stick
- Floral foam to fit pot
- Small alpine grit

Note

The succulent is worked in spirals using the standard amigurumi technique (see page 126). Place a marker at the beginning of each round so you know where you are in the pattern.

Succulent

Using 3.5mm (UK9:USE/4) hook, make a magic ring (see page 127).

Round 1: 1 ch, 6 dc into the centre of the ring.

Round 2: 2 dc into each st (12 sts).

Round 3: (1 dc, dc2inc) 6 times (18 sts).

Round 4: (2 dc, dc2inc) 6 times (24 sts).

Round 5: (3 dc, dc2inc) 6 times (30 sts).

Round 6: (4 dc, dc2inc) 6 times (36 sts).

Round 7: (5 dc, dc2inc) 6 times (42 sts).

Rounds 8–12: Work 5 rounds straight.

Round 13: (5 dc, dc2tog) 6 times (36 sts).

Round 14: (4 dc, dc2tog) 6 times (30 sts).

Round 15: (3 dc, dc2tog) 6 times (24 sts).

Round 16: (2 dc, dc2tog) 6 times (18 sts).

Stuff firmly with polyester stuffing.

Round 17: (1 dc, dc2tog) 6 times (12 sts).

Round 18: (Dc2tog) 6 times (6 sts).

Fasten off. Leave a yarn tail to create the segments.

Tip

Why not make a collection of plants in different shades of green? They will look very stylish arranged as a group and it's a great way to use up your yarn stash.

actual size

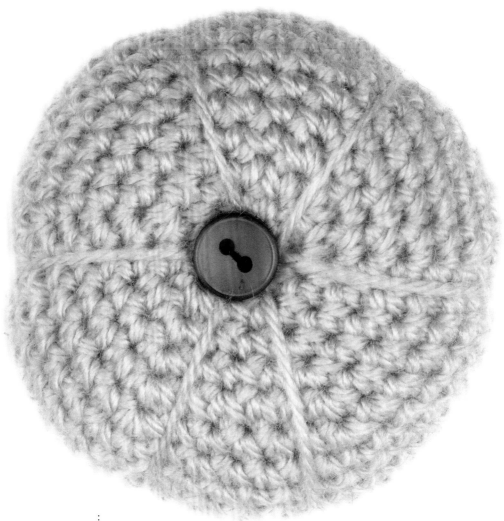

Making up

Use the tail of yarn to create segments. Bring your tapestry needle up through the base to the top of the plant. Pull the yarn around the outside of the succulent and push the needle back in at the centre of the base. Repeat this 5 times, spacing the segments evenly. For added detail, you can sew a small button in the centre of the plant. You could also add some sewing pins to the succulent to create spines and use the piece as an attractive pin cushion.

Place a cocktail stick through the base of the succulent. Cut some floral foam to fit your pot and stick the cocktail stick in. Then fill up the sides with small alpine grit. Or you can crochet a pot using one of the patterns on page 138. Alternatively crochet some soil to fit the pot using the pattern for the appropriate sized pot on page 137. Using the yarn tail from the succulent, sew the succulent firmly to the soil and place in the pot.

Saguaro

The saguaro has a very typical shape, the kind everyone thinks of if they imagine a cactus. Native to the deserts of Mexico and Arizona, it can grow up to 40ft (12m) tall. This crocheted version is rather smaller, and includes crocheted soil so it is all complete, ready to pop into a pot.

FINISHED SIZE

The cactus is approximately 4in (10cm) tall and 2½in (6cm) wide.

YOU WILL NEED

- Scheepjes Catona, 100% cotton (137yd/125m per 50g ball): 1 ball in 512 Lime (A)
- Scheepjes Catona, 100% cotton (27yd/25m per 10g ball): Small amount in 157 Root Beer (B)
- 3.5mm (UK9:USE/4) crochet hook
- Polyester stuffing
- Tapestry needle
- Floristry wire
- Plant pot approximately 2½in (6cm) in diameter

TENSION

Tension is not essential for this project.

Note

The cactus is worked in spirals using the standard amigurumi technique (see page 126). Place a marker at the beginning of each round so you know where you are in the pattern.

Cactus and soil

Using 3.5mm (UK9:USE/4) hook and A, make a magic ring (see page 127).

Round 1: 1 ch, 6 dc into the centre of the ring.

Round 2: 2 dc into each st (12 sts).

Round 3: (1 dc, dc2inc) 6 times (18 sts).

Round 4: (2 dc, dc2inc) 6 times (24 sts).

Round 5: (3 dc, dc2inc) 6 times (30 sts).

Round 6: (4 dc, dc2inc) 6 times (36 sts).

Rounds 7–16: Work 10 rounds straight.

Round 17: (4 dc, dc2tog) 6 times (30 sts).

Rounds 18–20: Work 3 rounds straight (30 sts).

Round 21: (3 dc, dc2tog) 6 times (24 sts).

Rounds 22–24: Work 3 rounds straight (24 sts).

Round 25: Change to yarn B. Work 1 round straight (24 sts).

Round 26: (3 dc, dc2inc) 6 times (30 sts).

Rounds 27–31: Work 5 rounds straight.

Round 32: (3 dc, dc2tog) 6 times (24 sts).

Round 33: (2 dc, dc2tog) 6 times (18 sts).

Round 34: (1 dc, dc2tog) 6 times (12 sts).

Round 35: (Dc2tog) 6 times (6 sts).

Fasten off.

actual size

Small cactus pieces (make 2)

Using 3.5mm (UK9:USE/4) hook and A, make a magic ring (see page 127).
Round 1: 1 ch, 6 dc into the centre of the ring.
Round 2: 2 dc into each st (12 sts).
Rounds 3–6: Work 4 rounds straight.
Round 7: (1 dc, dc2tog) 4 times (8 sts).
Fasten off. Leave a yarn tail.

Making up

Firmly stuff the main part of the cactus and the soil with polyester stuffing. Cut a piece of floristry wire so it is just longer than one of the small pieces of cactus. Stuff the small pieces of cactus and then place a piece of floristry wire into the middle. Poke the end of the wire into the main cactus and then sew the crochet of the small pieces to the main cactus. You can then bend the small pieces upwards to create that distinct Mexican cactus look.

Place in a plant pot or crochet a pot using one of the patterns on page 138.

Mexican Giant Cardon

The flowers of this plant, which is also known as the elephant cactus, are usually white, but here I made one in bright yellow to introduce some vibrant colour. The distinctive ridges of its trunk are recreated with a crocheted rib stitch.

FINISHED SIZE

The cactus is approximately 3in (8cm) tall and 2in (5cm) in diameter.

YOU WILL NEED

- Stylecraft Special DK, 100% acrylic (323yd/295m per 100g ball):
  1 ball in 1826 Kelly Green (A)
  Small amount in 1081 Saffron (B)
  1 ball in 1054 Walnut (C)
- 3.5mm (UK9:USE/4) crochet hook
- Polyester stuffing
- Tapestry needle
- Plant pot approximately 2½in (6cm) in diameter

TENSION

Tension is not essential for this project.

Note

The cactus is worked in rows. The rib is created by working into the back loop of each stitch (see page 131).

Cactus

Row 1: Using 3.5mm (UK9:USE/4) hook and A, ch 17 sts.

Row 2 WS: 1 dc in 2nd ch from hook, dc into each ch to end, turn (16 sts).

Row 3: Ch 1, dc tbl into each st to end, turn (16 sts).

Row 3 forms the pattern.

Work a further 18 rows.

With RS together now crochet the first and last rows together:

Next row: Ch1, sl st in every st.

Fasten off and leave a long yarn tail.

actual size

Spiky flower (make 1)

Using 3.5mm (UK9:USE/4) hook and B, make a magic ring (see page 127).

Round 1: 1 ch, 9 dc into the centre of the ring, join with a sl st.

Round 2: (Ch 4, miss 1 ch, 1 sl st along the rest of ch sts, sl st in same st),
* sl st in next st, 4 ch, miss 1 ch, 1 sl st along the rest of ch sts, sl st in same st; rep from * 7 times.

Fasten off. Leave a yarn tail.

Soil

Using 3.5mm (UK9:USE/4) hook and C, make a magic ring (see page 127).

Round 1: 1 ch, 6 dc into the centre of the ring.

Round 2: 2 dc into each st (12 sts).

Round 3: (1 dc, dc2inc) 6 times (18 sts).

Round 4: (2 dc, dc2inc) 6 times (24 sts).

Round 5: 1 dc in each st tbl (24 sts).

Rounds 6–12: Work 7 rounds straight.

Round 13: (2 dc, dc2tog) 6 times (18 sts). Stuff firmly with polyester stuffing.

Round 14: (1 dc, dc2tog) 6 times (12 sts).

Round 15: (Dc2tog) 6 times (6 sts).

Using a tapestry needle, weave this yarn through the last dc sts of the round and gather hole together. Fasten off and weave in ends.

Making up

Along one side seam, use the yarn tail to sew small running stitches and then gather the end together to form the top of the cactus. Firmly stuff the cactus. Sew the flower to the top of the cactus. Using the yarn tail, sew the bottom of the cactus firmly to the crocheted soil. Alternatively, insert a cocktail stick through the base of the cactus. Cut some floral foam to fit the pot and push the cocktail stick into the foam to secure the cactus in the pot. Then fill up the sides with small alpine grit.

Moulded Wax Agave

Native to Mexico, this small succulent,
which can grow to about 8in (20cm) in diameter, is relatively
easy to cultivate even in Europe. It is recognizable for its attractive
rosette-type structure, which, with a little sewing together,
is easy to reproduce in crocheted form.

FINISHED SIZE

The succulent is approximately 2¾in (7cm) in diameter.

TENSION

Tension is not essential for this project.

YOU WILL NEED

- Scheepjes Catona, 100% cotton (137yd/125m per 50g ball):
  1 ball in 512 Lime
- 3.5mm (UK9:USE/4) crochet hook
- Tapestry needle
- Floristry wire
- Floral foam to fit pot
- Small alpine grit
- Plant pot approximately 3½in (9cm) in diameter

Note

The succulent leaves are worked in spirals using the standard amigurumi technique (see page 126). Place a marker at the beginning of each round so you know where you are in the pattern. You then sew the leaves together to create the whole plant.

Large leaf (make 10)

Using 3.5mm (UK9:USE/4) hook, make a magic ring (see page 127).
Round 1: 1 ch, 6 dc into the centre of the ring.
Round 2: (2 dc, dc2inc) twice (8 sts).
Round 3: (3 dc, dc2inc) twice (10 sts).
Rounds 4–9: Work 6 rounds straight.
Round 10: (3 dc, dc2tog) twice (8 sts).
Round 11: (2 dc, dc2tog) twice (6 sts).
Fasten off. Leave a yarn tail.

Small leaf (make 3)

Using 3.5mm hook (UK9:USE/4), make a magic ring (see page 127).
Round 1: 1 ch, 4 dc into the centre of the ring.
Round 2: (1 dc, dc2inc) twice (6 sts).
Round 3: (2 dc, dc2inc) twice (8 sts).
Rounds 4–7: Work 4 rounds straight.
Round 8: (2 dc, dc2tog) twice (6 sts).
Fasten off. Leave a yarn tail.

Centre leaves

Using 3.5mm (UK9:USE/4) hook, make a magic ring (see page 127).
Round 1: 1 ch, 6 dc into the centre of the ring, join with a sl st.
Round 2: (Ch 2, sl st in next st), *sl st into next st, 2 ch, sl st in next st; rep from * (3 loops).
Round 3: *Sl st in ch sp, (2 ch, 3 tr, 2 ch, 1 sl st) in ch sp; rep from * twice (3 petals).
Fasten off. Leave a yarn tail.

actual size

Making up

Fold each leaf in half and press it
flat with your hand. Arrange five
large leaves to form a flat star,
then, using the tail of yarn, sew
the end rows together. Repeat
with the other five large leaves
so you have two flat stars of five
leaves each. Sew one star of
leaves on top of the other, making
sure the leaves are staggered.
Then space the three small
leaves equally to form a trefoil,
sew these together and then sew
them on top of your large leaves.
Finally, sew the small centre
leaves right in the middle.

Take some floristry wire, fold
it in half and thread it through
the centre underside of the
succulent. Cut some floral foam
to fit the pot. Insert the floristry
wire into the foam to secure the
plant in the pot. Add some small
alpine grit to cover the foam.

San Pedro

This cactus grows at high altitudes in the Andes Mountains and has a long tradition of being used in healing and herbal medicine. Its flowers are usually white, but I made a colourful pompom for a more fanciful touch.

FINISHED SIZE

The cactus is approximately 4in (10cm) tall and 2¾in (7cm) wide.

TENSION

Tension is not essential for this project.

YOU WILL NEED

- Robin Double Knit, 100% acrylic (328yd/300m per 100g ball):
  1 ball in 045 Forest (A)
  1 ball in 143 Mink (B)
  Small amount of yarn in colour of your choice to make pompom
- 3.5mm (UK9:USE/4) crochet hook
- Polyester stuffing
- Tapestry needle
- Fork (to make pompom)
- Cocktail stick
- Plant pot approximately 2½in (6cm) in diameter

Note

The cactus is worked in spirals using the standard amigurumi technique (see page 126). Place a marker at the beginning of each round so you know where you are in the pattern.

Cactus

Using 3.5mm (UK9:USE/4) hook and A, make a magic ring (see page 127).

Round 1: 1 ch, 6 dc into the centre of the ring.

Round 2: 2 dc into each st (12 sts).

Round 3: (1 dc, dc2inc) 6 times (18 sts).

Round 4: (2 dc, dc2inc) 6 times (24 sts).

Round 5: (3 dc, dc2inc) 6 times (30 sts).

Round 6: (4 dc, dc2inc) 6 times (36 sts).

Round 7: (5 dc, dc2inc) 6 times (42 sts).

Round 8: (6 dc, dc2inc) 6 times (48 sts).

Rounds 9–16: Work 8 rounds straight.

Round 17: (6 dc, dc2tog) 6 times (42 sts).

Rounds 18–19: Work 2 rounds straight (42 sts).

Round 20: (5 dc, dc2tog) 6 times (36 sts).

Round 21: Work 1 round straight (36 sts).

Round 22: (4 dc, dc2tog) 6 times (30 sts).

Round 23: Work 1 round straight (30 sts).

Round 24: (3 dc, dc2tog) 6 times (24 sts).

Round 25: Work 1 round straight (24 sts).

Round 26: (2 dc, dc2tog) 6 times (18 sts).

Round 27: Work 1 round straight (18 sts).

Round 28: (1 dc, dc2tog) 6 times (12 sts).

Round 29: (Dc2tog) 6 times (6 sts).

Fasten off. Leave a yarn tail to sew to the soil.

actual size

Soil

Using 3.5mm (UK9:USE/4) hook and B, make a magic ring (see page 127).

Round 1: 1 ch, 6 dc into the centre of the ring.

Round 2: 2 dc into each st (12 sts).

Round 3: (1 dc, dc2inc) 6 times (18 sts).

Round 4: (2 dc, dc2inc) 6 times (24 sts).

Round 5: 1 dc in each st tbl (24 sts).

Rounds 6–12: Work 7 rounds straight.

Round 13: (2 dc, dc2tog) 6 times (18 sts). Stuff firmly with polyester stuffing.

Round 14: (1 dc, dc2tog) 6 times (12 sts).

Round 15: (Dc2tog) 6 times (6 sts).

Using a tapestry needle, weave this yarn through the last dc sts of the round and gather hole together. Fasten off and weave in ends.

Making up

Pinch together the cactus to make four folds in the sides. Then, using yarn A and your tapestry needle, sew some small stitches through both sides of the crochet to hold the folds together. Insert a cocktail stick up through the base of the cactus, so that half of the stick is in the cactus and half is poking out. This will ensure the cactus remains upright. Then poke the end of the stick into the crocheted soil piece. Using the yarn tail from the cactus, sew firmly to the crocheted soil. Using some remnants of yarn, use the fork technique to make a pompom (see page 135) and sew it firmly to the top of the cactus. You can crochet a pot for the cactus using one of the patterns on page 138 or place the finished piece in a small terracotta pot.

Jade Necklace

This small succulent is very distinctive-looking, with small, star-shaped leaves that grow in trailing clusters – here recreated in many strands of spiral crochet that are sewn together. If you use a variegated yarn you can achieve different tones.

FINISHED SIZE

The longest spiral is approximately 6½in (16cm) long.

TENSION

Tension is not essential for this project.

YOU WILL NEED

- Scheepjes Secret Garden, 60% polyester, 20% silk, 20% cotton (102yd/93m per 50g ball):
  1 ball in 702 Herb Garden
- 3.5mm (UK9:USE/4) crochet hook
- Tapestry needle
- Floral foam to fit pot
- Square of brown felt approximately 6 x 6in (15 x 15cm)
- Craft glue
- Plant pot approximately 2½in (6cm) in diameter

Note

The spirals are worked separately and then sewn together when assembled at the end.

Large spiral
(make 4)

Row 1: Using 3.5mm (UK9:USE/4) hook, ch 34 sts.
Row 2: 1 tr in 4th ch from hook, 4 tr into each ch to end.
Fasten off and leave a long yarn tail.

The crochet will naturally spiral, but to achieve an even look, twist the length of the spiral around your fingers.

Medium spiral
(make 4)

Row 1: Using 3.5mm (UK9:USE/4) hook, ch 24 sts.
Row 2: 1 tr in 4th ch from hook, 4 tr into each ch to end.
Fasten off and leave a long yarn tail.

Small spiral
(make 1)

Row 1: Using 3.5mm (UK9:USE/4) hook, ch 14 sts.
Row 2: 1 tr in 4th ch from hook, 4 tr into each ch to end.
Fasten off and leave a long yarn tail.

actual size

Making up

Evenly sew the spirals together
at the ends using the yarn tails.
Cut a piece of floral foam to fit
your pot. Fold the brown felt over
the foam so that it smoothly
covers the top to form soil. Using
craft glue, stick the felt to the
sides of the foam. Place the
felt-covered foam into your pot.
Then sew the attached spirals
firmly to the centre of the felt soil.
Space out and arrange the
spirals so they cascade naturally
over the edge of the pot.

Red Frills

This succulent can grow up to 12in (30cm) in diameter and is notable for its spectacular colours and gorgeous crinkly, frilly edges. The real colour can be dark red or burgundy, but here I chose a vibrant fuchsia.

FINISHED SIZE

The succulent is approximately 3¼in (8cm) in diameter.

TENSION

Tension is not essential for this project.

YOU WILL NEED

- Scheepjes Catona, 100% cotton (137yd/125m per 50g ball):
  1 ball in 205 Kiwi (A)
  1 ball in 192 Scarlet (B)
- 3mm (UK11:US–) crochet hook
- Tapestry needle
- Floral foam to fit pot
- Floristry wire
- Plant pot approximately 3¼in (8cm) in diameter

Note

The succulent is worked in spirals using the standard amigurumi technique (see page 126). Place a marker at the beginning of each round so you know where you are in the pattern.

Frills

Using 3mm (UK11:US–) hook and A, make a magic ring (see page 127).

Round 1: 1 ch, 6 dc into the centre of the ring.

Round 2: 2 dc into each st (12 sts).

Round 3: 2 dc into each st (24 sts).

Round 4: 2 dc into each st (48 sts).

Round 5: 2 dc into each st (96 sts).

Round 6: 2 dc into each st (192 sts).

Round 7: 2 dc into each st (384 sts).

Fasten off A and weave in ends.

Round 8: Change to B, 1 ch, 1 dc in each st around.

Fasten off and weave in ends.

actual size

Making up

Arrange the frills so the maximum number of folds is on display. Using the tapestry needle and yarn A, make a few small stitches in the centre of the succulent to secure the shape. Cut some floral foam to fit the pot. Take some floristry wire, fold it in half and thread it through the centre underside of the succulent. Then insert the wire into the foam to secure the plant in the pot.

Alternatively, make some crocheted soil to fit a plant pot 3¼in (8cm) in diameter (see pattern on page 137). Sew the very centre of the succulent firmly to the crocheted soil and place it in the pot.

Golden Barrel

Obviously this cactus derives its common name from its barrel-shaped form. The real version is covered in spines, which gave rise to another, rather unfriendly, common name of 'mother-in-law's cushion'. This more cuddly version is worked in rows to create the ridged effect, and can be made in two sizes.

FINISHED SIZES

The small cactus is approximately 3in (8cm) in diameter; the large one is approximately 8in (20cm).

YOU WILL NEED

For the small version:

- Stylecraft Special DK, 100% acrylic (323yd/295m per 100g ball): 1 ball in 904 Meadow
- 3.5mm (UK9:USE/4) crochet hook
- ⅝in (15mm) button
- Sewing needle and thread
- Cocktail stick
- Polyester stuffing
- Tapestry needle
- Floral foam to fit pot
- Small alpine grit
- Plant pot approximately 2in (5cm) in diameter

For the large version:

- Stylecraft Special XL super chunky, 100% acrylic (149yd/136m per 200g ball): 1 ball in 1712 Lime (A)
- Stylecraft Special DK, 100% acrylic (323yd/295m per 100g ball): Small amount in 1083 Pomegranate (B)
- 5mm (UK6:USH/8) crochet hook
- 10mm (UK000:USN-P/15) crochet hook
- Wooden skewer
- Polyester stuffing
- Tapestry needle
- Floral foam to fit pot
- Small alpine grit
- Plant pot approximately 4in (10cm) in diameter

TENSION

Tension is not essential for this project.

Note

The cactus is worked in rows. The rib is created by working into the back loop of each stitch (see page 131).

Small cactus

Row 1: Using 3.5mm (UK9:USE/4) hook, ch 21 sts.

Row 2 WS: 1 htr in 3rd ch from hook, htr into each ch to end, turn (19 sts).

Row 3: Ch 2, htr tbl into each st to end, turn (19 sts).

Row 3 forms the pattern. Work a further 26 rows.

With RS together now crochet the first and last rows together:

Next row: Ch1, sl st in every st.

Fasten off and leave a long yarn tail.

Large cactus

Row 1: Using 10mm (UK000:USN-P/15) hook and A, ch 21 sts.

Row 2 WS: 1 htr in 3rd ch from hook, htr into each ch to end, turn (19 sts).

Row 3: Ch 2, htr tbl into each st to end, turn (19 sts).

Row 3 forms the pattern. Work a further 26 rows.

With RS together now crochet the first and last rows together.

Next row: Ch 1, sl st in every st.

Fasten off and leave a long yarn tail.

Flower

Using 5mm (UK6:USH/8) hook and holding yarn B double, make a magic ring (see page 127).

Round 1: 1 ch, 5 dc into the centre of the ring, join with a sl st.

Round 2: (Ch 2, 2 tr, 2 ch, sl st), in first st, * sl st in next st, 2 ch, 2 tr, 2 ch, sl st in same st; rep from * 3 times.

Fasten off. Leave a long yarn tail.

actual size

Making up

Use the yarn tail and tapestry needle to make small running stitches along both side seams. Gather one end then firmly stuff the cactus with polyester stuffing. Gather the other end to close. Sew the button to the top of the small cactus and pull the needle down through the stuffing. Secure to the base of the cactus so that it creates an indentation on top.

Sew the flower to the top of the large cactus and pull the needle down through the stuffing.

Cut some floral foam to fit your pots. Poke a cocktail stick through the base of the small cactus and a skewer through the large one. Secure the cacti in their pots by inserting the sticks into the foam. Fill the sides with small alpine grit. Alternatively, for the small cactus, crochet some

soil to fit a plant pot 2½in (6cm) in diameter (see pattern on page 137). Using the yarn tail from the cactus, sew the cactus firmly to the soil and place in the pot. You can also crochet a pot for the small cactus using one of the patterns on page 138.

Notocactus

This small cactus is native to Brazil and is often found growing in cracks in rocks or walls. Its distinctive spikes are here recreated using a tinsel or eyelash yarn and crocheting rows on top of a crocheted base.

FINISHED SIZE

The cactus is approximately 3½in (9cm) in diameter.

TENSION

Tension is not essential for this project.

YOU WILL NEED

- Robin Double Knit, 100% acrylic (328yd/300m per 100g ball): 1 ball in 045 Forest (A)
- Rico Design Creative Bubble, 100% polyester (98yd/90m 50g ball): 1 ball in 013 Iridescent White (B)
- 3.5mm (UK9:USE/4) crochet hook
- Polyester stuffing
- Tapestry needle
- Cocktail stick
- Floral foam to fit pot
- Small alpine grit
- Plant pot approximately 2½in (6cm) in diameter

Note

The cactus is worked in rows. The rib is created by working into the back loop of each stitch (see page 131).

Cactus

Row 1: Using 3.5mm (UK9:USE/4) hook and A, ch 21 sts.

Row 2 WS: 1 htr in 3rd ch from hook, htr into each ch to end, turn (19 sts).

Row 3: Ch 2, htr tbl into each st to end, turn (19 sts).

Row 3 forms the pattern.

Work a further 26 rows.

With RS together, crochet the first and last rows together:

Next row: Ch 1, sl st in every st.

Fasten off and leave a long yarn tail.

Tip

Using eyelash yarn can sometimes prove tricky, so crochet in good light and use your fingers to feel where the next hole is for your next stitch. But don't worry too much – eyelash yarn is also very forgiving as it will cover up any missed stitches!

Spikes

Using B, with RS facing, crochet along the ridges created by the htr. Attach the yarn using a sl st and double crochet in each stitch. Fasten off. You will complete 14 rows of spikes.

actual size

Making up

Use a yarn tail and tapestry
needle to make small running
stitches along both side seams.
Gather one end then firmly stuff
the cactus with polyester stuffing.
Gather the other end to close.
Cut some floral foam to fit the pot.
Poke a cocktail stick through the
cactus base, then insert the stick
into the foam to secure the
cactus in the pot. Then fill up the
sides with small alpine grit.

Alternatively, crochet some soil
to fit a pot 2½in (6cm) in diameter
using the pattern on page 137.
Using the yarn tail from the
cactus, sew the plant firmly to
the soil. Place in a small pot or
you can crochet a pot for the
cactus using one of the patterns
on page 138.

Little Mouse

This small globe-shaped cactus is covered in spines, which I recreated in this pattern by using two strands of yarn held together. The soft merino gives the colour, while the silk and mohair mix yarn provides the furry halo.

FINISHED SIZE

Large cactus is approximately 1¾in (4.5cm) in diameter.
Small cactus is approximately ¾in (2cm) in diameter.

TENSION

Tension is not essential for this project.

YOU WILL NEED

- Scheepjes Alpaca Rhythm, 80% alpaca, 20% wool (219yd/200m per 25g ball):
  1 ball in 654 Robotic (A)
  1 ball in 607 Braque (B)
- Rowan Kidsilk Haze, 70% super kid mohair, 30% silk (230yd/210m per 25g ball):
  1 ball in 642 Ghost (C)
- 3mm (UK11:US–) crochet hook
- Polyester stuffing
- Tapestry needle
- Plant pot approximately 2½in (6cm) in diameter

Note

The cacti are worked in spirals using the standard amigurumi technique (see page 126). Place a marker at the beginning of each round so you know where you are in the pattern. You can then sew them together to create the whole plant.

Large cactus (make 1)

Using 3mm (UK11:US–) hook and with strands of A and C held together, make a magic ring (see page 127).

Round 1: 1 ch, 6 dc into the centre of the ring.

Round 2: 2 dc into each st (12 sts).

Round 3: (1 dc, dc2inc) 6 times (18 sts).

Round 4: (2 dc, dc2inc) 6 times (24 sts).

Round 5: (3 dc, dc2inc) 6 times (30 sts).

Rounds 6–9: Work 4 rounds straight.

Round 10: (3 dc, dc2tog) 6 times (24 sts).

Round 11: (2 dc, dc2tog) 6 times (18 sts).

Round 12: (1 dc, dc2tog) 6 times (12 sts). Stuff with a small amount of polyester stuffing.

Round 13: (Dc2tog) 6 times (6 sts).

Using a tapestry needle, weave this yarn through the last dc sts of the round and gather hole together. Fasten off. Leave a long yarn tail to sew to the other cacti.

Medium cactus (make 1)

Using 3mm (UK11:US–) hook and with strands of A and C held together, make a magic ring (see page 127).

Round 1: 1 ch, 6 dc into the centre of the ring.

Round 2: 2 dc into each st (12 sts).

Round 3: (2 dc, dc2inc) 4 times (16 sts).

Rounds 4–5: Work 2 rounds straight.

Round 6: (2 dc, dc2tog) 4 times (12 sts). Stuff with a small amount of polyester stuffing.

Round 7: (Dc2tog) 6 times (6 sts).

Using a tapestry needle, weave this yarn through the last dc sts of the round and gather hole together. Fasten off.

Mini cacti (make 2)

Using 3mm (UK11:US–) hook and with strands of A and C held together, make a magic ring (see page 127).

Round 1: 1 ch, 6 dc into the centre of the ring.

Round 2: 2 dc into each st (12 sts).

Rounds 3–4: Work 2 rounds straight. Stuff with a small amount of polyester stuffing.

Round 5: (Dc2tog) 6 times (6 sts).

Using a tapestry needle, weave this yarn through the last dc sts of the round and gather hole together. Fasten off.

actual size

Soil

Using 3.5mm (UK9:USE/4) hook and B, make a magic ring (see page 127).

Round 1: 1 ch, 6 dc into the centre of the ring.

Round 2: 2 dc into each st (12 sts).

Round 3: (1 dc, dc2inc) 6 times (18 sts).

Round 4: (2 dc, dc2inc) 6 times (24 sts).

Round 5: 1 dc in each st tbl (24 sts).

Rounds 6–12: Work 7 rounds straight.

Round 13: (2 dc, dc2tog) 6 times (18 sts). Stuff firmly with polyester stuffing.

Round 14: (1 dc, dc2tog) 6 times (12 sts).

Round 15: (Dc2tog) 6 times (6 sts). Using a tapestry needle, weave this yarn through the last dc sts of the round and gather hole together. Fasten off and weave in ends.

Making up

Using the tapestry needle and the yarn tail from the large cactus, sew all four cacti together. Then stitch them firmly to the soil. Alternatively, cut a piece of floral foam to fit your pot. Push a cocktail stick halfway into the base of the large cactus piece. Then push the cocktail stick into the foam to secure the cactus in the pot. Add small alpine grit to cover the foam.

Romeo Wax Agave

In real life, this pretty succulent tends to be a more subtle shade of purple or red, but when you are crocheting you can use as bright a pink or red as you fancy to add some colour variety to your cactus collection.

FINISHED SIZE

The succulent is approximately 4½in (11cm) in diameter.

TENSION

Tension is not essential for this project.

YOU WILL NEED

- Scheepjes Catona, 100% cotton (137yd/125m per 50g ball): 1 ball in 517 Ruby
- 3.5mm (UK9:USE/4) crochet hook
- Tapestry needle
- Floristry wire
- Floral foam to fit pot
- Plant pot approximately 3in (7.5cm) in diameter

Note

The succulent is worked in rounds: you start in the centre and then build the round of leaves below.

Large leaf
(make 6)

Using 3.5mm (UK9:USE/4) hook, make
a magic ring (see page 127).

Round 1: 1 ch, 4 dc into the centre of
the ring.
Round 2: (Dc2inc) four times (8 sts).
Round 3: (3 dc, dc2inc) twice (10 sts).
Round 4: (4 dc, dc2inc) twice (12 sts).
Round 5: (5 dc, dc2inc) twice (14 sts).
Round 6: (6 dc, dc2inc) twice (16 sts).
Round 7: (7 dc, dc2inc) twice (18 sts).
Rounds 8–9: Work 2 rounds straight.
Round 10: (1 dc, dc2tog) six times
(12 sts).
Round 11: (Dc2tog) six times (6 sts).
Fasten off. Leave a yarn tail.

Small leaf
(make 3)

Using 3.5mm (UK9:USE/4) hook,
make a magic ring (see page 127).

Round 1: 1 ch, 4 dc into the centre
of the ring.
Round 2: (Dc2inc) four times (8 sts).
Round 3: (3 dc, dc2inc) twice (10 sts).
Round 4: (4 dc, dc2inc) twice (12 sts).
Round 5: (5 dc, dc2inc) twice (14 sts).
Rounds 6–7: Work 2 rounds straight.
Round 8: (1 dc, dc2tog) four times,
2 dc (10 sts).
Round 9: (Dc2tog) five times (5 sts).
Fasten off. Leave a yarn tail.

Centre leaves

Using 3.5mm (UK9:USE/4) hook, make
a magic ring (see page 127).

Round 1: 1 ch, 6 dc into the centre of
the ring, join with a sl st.
Round 2: (Ch 2, sl st in next st), *sl st
into next st, 2 ch, sl st in next st; rep
from * (3 loops).
Round 3: *Sl st in ch sp, (2 ch, 1 tr, 2 ch,
1 sl st in first ch, 1 tr, 2 ch, 1 sl st) in ch
sp; rep from * twice (3 leaves).
Fasten off. Leave a yarn tail.

actual size

Making up

Fold each leaf in half and press it flat with your hand. Arrange three large leaves to form a star shape. Using the tail of yarn and the tapestry needle, sew the end rows together to form a flat star. Sew another star made up of three leaves. Sew one star of leaves on top of the other, making sure the leaves are staggered. Then space the three small leaves out evenly to form a trefoil. Sew these together, then sew them on top of your large leaves. Finally, sew the small centre leaves right in the middle. Take some floristry wire, fold in half and thread through the centre underside of the succulent. Cut some floral foam to fit the pot and insert the wire into the foam to secure the plant in the pot.

Aloe Vera

This popular plant has long been known for the medicinal properties of its juice, which is used to soothe burns and skin irritation. The leaves can grow up to 2ft (60cm) tall, but this crocheted version is made to a more shelf-friendly scale.

FINISHED SIZE

Each leaf is approximately 4½in (11cm) tall.

YOU WILL NEED

- James C. Brett Cotton On, 50% cotton, 50% acrylic (159yd/145m per 50g ball): 1 ball in 16 Lime
- 3.5mm (UK9:USE/4) crochet hook
- Floristry wire
- Tapestry needle
- Cocktail sticks
- Floral foam to fit pot
- Small alpine grit
- Plant pot approximately 4½in (11cm) in diameter

TENSION

Tension is not essential for this project.

Note

The succulent leaves are worked in spirals using the standard amigurumi technique (see page 126). Place a marker at the beginning of each round so you know where you are in the pattern. You can then sew the leaves together to create the whole plant.

Large leaf
(make 11)

Using 3.5mm (UK9:USE/4) hook, make a magic ring (see page 127).

Round 1: 1 ch, 4 dc into the centre of the ring.

Round 2: 1 dc in each st (4 sts).

Round 3: 3 dc, dc2inc (5 sts).

Rounds 4–5: Work 2 rounds straight.

Round 6: 4 dc, dc2inc (6 sts).

Rounds 7–10: Work 4 rounds straight.

Round 11: 5 dc, dc2inc (7 sts).

Rounds 12–16: Work 5 rounds straight.

Round 17: 6 dc, dc2inc (8 sts).

Rounds 18–21: Work 4 rounds straight.

Round 22: 7 dc, dc2inc (9 sts).

Rounds 23–24: Work 2 rounds straight.

Fasten off. Leave a yarn tail.

actual size

Making up

Place a piece of floristry wire in each leaf so that you can bend and arrange the leaf to suit your arrangement. Arrange three leaves together to form the centre and sew them firmly together at the base. Then sew on the other leaves to the outside of the centre leaves, making sure the leaves overlap. Take some skewers and insert one in the centre of the plant and three on outer leaves.

Cut some floral foam to fit the pot and poke the cocktail sticks into the foam to secure the plant in the pot. Fill the top of the pot with small alpine grit to cover the floral foam.

Bunny Ears Cactus

This cactus, native to Mexico and Arizona, grows up to 2ft (60cm) tall. It has no central stem but each oval-shaped segment grows from another segment. Its spines can be painful, and are here recreated in less formidable form by sewing small seed beads onto the crocheted base.

FINISHED SIZE

The cactus is approximately 4in (10cm) tall and 2in (4cm) wide.

TENSION

Tension is not essential for this project.

YOU WILL NEED

- Scheepjes Catona, 100% cotton (127yd/125m per 50g ball): 1 ball in 244 Spruce (A)
- Scheepjes Catona, 100% cotton (27yd/25m per 10g ball): 1 ball in 157 Root Beer (B)
- 3.5mm (UK9:USE/4) crochet hook
- Polyester stuffing
- Tapestry needle
- Approximately 100 white seed beads
- Black sewing thread
- Beading needle
- Cocktail stick
- Plant pot approximately 2½in (6cm) in diameter

Note

The cactus is worked in spirals using the standard amigurumi technique (see page 126). Place a marker at the beginning of each round so you know where you are in the pattern

Large leaf

Using 3.5mm (UK9:USE/4) hook and A, make a magic ring (see page 127).

Round 1: 1 ch, 5 dc into the centre of the ring.

Round 2: 2 dc into each st (10 sts).

Round 3: (4 dc, dc2inc) rep (12 sts).

Round 4: (5 dc, dc2inc) rep (14 sts).

Round 5: (6 dc, dc2inc) rep (16 sts).

Round 6: (7 dc, dc2inc) rep (18 sts).

Round 7: (8 dc, dc2inc) rep (20 sts).

Round 8: (9 dc, dc2inc) rep (22 sts).

Rounds 9–11: Work 3 rounds straight.

Round 12: (9 dc, dc2tog) rep (20 sts).

Round 13: Work 1 round straight (20 sts).

Round 14: (8 dc, dc2tog) rep (18 sts).

Round 15: Work 1 round straight (18 sts).

Round 16: (7 dc, dc2tog) rep (16 sts).

Round 17: Work 1 round straight (16 sts).

Round 18: (6 dc, dc2tog) rep (14 sts).

Round 19: Work 1 round straight (14 sts).

Round 20: (5 dc, dc2tog) rep (12 sts).

Round 21: Work 1 round straight (12 sts).

Round 22: (4 dc, dc2tog) rep (10 sts). Fasten off. Leave a yarn tail to sew to the soil.

Medium leaf

Using 3.5mm (UK9:USE/4) hook and A, make a magic ring (see page 127).

Round 1: 1 ch, 5 dc into the centre of the ring.

Round 2: 2 dc into each st (10 sts).

Round 3: (4 dc, dc2inc) rep (12 sts).

Round 4: (5 dc, dc2inc) rep (14 sts).

Round 5: (6 dc, dc2inc) rep (16 sts).

Round 6: (7 dc, dc2inc) rep (18 sts).

Round 7: (8 dc, dc2inc) rep (20 sts).

Rounds 8–10: Work 3 rounds straight.

Round 11: (8 dc, dc2tog) rep (18 sts).

Round 12: Work 1 round straight (18 sts).

Round 13: (7 dc, dc2tog) rep (16 sts).

Round 14: Work 1 round straight (16 sts).

Round 15: (6 dc, dc2tog) rep (14 sts).

Round 16: Work 1 round straight (14 sts).

Round 17: (5 dc, dc2tog) rep (12 sts).

Round 18: Work 1 round straight (12 sts).

Round 19: (4 dc, dc2tog) rep (10 sts). Fasten off. Leave a yarn tail to sew to the soil.

actual size

Small leaf

Using 3.5mm (UK9:USE/4) hook and A,
make a magic ring (see page 127).

Round 1: 1 ch, 5 dc into the centre of
the ring.

Round 2: 2 dc into each st (10 sts).

Round 3: (4 dc, dc2inc) rep (12 sts).

Round 4: (5 dc, dc2inc) rep (14 sts).

Rounds 5–6: Work 2 rounds straight.

Round 7: (5 dc, dc2tog) rep (12 sts).

Round 8: Work 1 round straight (12 sts).

Round 9: (4 dc, dc2tog) rep (10 sts).

Round 10: (Dc2tog) five times (5 sts).

Fasten off. Leave a yarn tail to sew to
the soil.

Soil

Using 3.5mm (UK9:USE/4) hook and B,
make a magic ring (see page 127).

Round 1: 1 ch, 6 dc into the centre of
the ring.

Round 2: 2 dc into each st (12 sts).

Round 3: (1 dc, dc2inc) 6 times (18 sts).

Round 4: (2 dc, dc2inc) 6 times (24 sts).

Round 5: 1 dc in each st tbl (24 sts).

Rounds 6–12: Work 7 rounds straight.

Round 13: (2 dc, dc2tog) 6 times
(18 sts).

Stuff firmly with polyester stuffing.

Round 14: (1 dc, dc2tog) 6 times
(12 sts).

Round 15: (Dc2tog) 6 times (6 sts).

Fasten off and weave in ends.

Making up

Flatten each leaf with the palm
of your hand. Using black
sewing thread and the beading
needle, sew white seed beads to
the surface of each leaf. As
a rough guide, you can sew a
bead on every third stitch on
each row: don't be too precise,
as a random pattern will look
more natural (see page 134 for
more on this technique).

Sew the small leaf on an edge of
the large leaf. Place a cocktail
stick through the base of both the
large leaf and the medium leaf,
then insert this stick through the
soil. Using the tails of yarn, sew
the plant firmly to the soil. Place
in a small plant pot.

Golden Torch

These cacti are native to South America, particularly Argentina. They can grow up to around 7ft (2m) tall. I have turned the crochet material inside out to create a different texture. The flowers are usually white, but here I made them in pink to add a touch of colour.

FINISHED SIZE

The large cactus is approximately 2¾in (7cm) tall.

TENSION

Tension is not essential for this project.

YOU WILL NEED

- Stylecraft Special DK, 100% acrylic (323yd/295m per 100g ball):
  1 ball in 904 Meadow (A)
  Small amount in 1833 Blush (B)
  1 ball in 1054 Walnut (C)
- 3.5mm (UK9:USE/4) crochet hook
- Polyester stuffing
- Tapestry needle
- Cocktail stick
- Floral foam to fit pot
- Small alpine grit
- Plant pot approximately 3½in (9cm) in diameter

Note

The cactus is worked in spirals using the standard amigurumi technique (see page 126). Place a marker at the beginning of each round so you know where you are in the pattern.

Tall cactus
(make 3)

Using 3.5mm (UK9:USE/4) hook and A, make a magic ring (see page 127).
Round 1: 1 ch, 6 dc into the centre of the ring, join with a sl st.
Round 2: 2 dc into each st (12 sts).
Round 3: (1 dc, dc2inc) 6 times (18 sts).
Rounds 4–18: Work 15 rounds straight. Fasten off. Leave a yarn tail.

Small cactus
(make 1)

Using 3.5mm (UK9:USE/4) hook and A, make a magic ring (see page 127).
Round 1: 1 ch, 6 dc into the centre of the ring, join with a sl st.
Round 2: 2 dc into each st (12 sts).
Round 3: (2 dc, dc2inc) 4 times (16 sts).
Rounds 4–11: Work 8 rounds straight. Fasten off. Leave a yarn tail.

Spiky flower
(make 2)

Using 3.5mm (UK9:USE/4) hook and B, make a magic ring (see page 127).
Round 1: 1 ch, 9 dc into the centre of the ring, join with a sl st.
Round 2: (Ch 4, miss 1 ch, 1 sl st along the rest of ch sts, sl st in same st), *sl st in next st, 4 ch, miss 1 ch, 1 sl st along the rest of ch sts, sl st in same st; rep from * 4 times.
Fasten off. Leave a yarn tail.

actual size

Flower bud (make 1)

Using 3.5mm (UK9:USE/4) hook and B, make a magic ring (see page 127).
Round 1: 1 ch, 6 dc into the centre of the ring, join with a sl st.
Fasten off. Leave a yarn tail.

Soil

Using 3.5mm (UK9:USE/4) hook and C, make a magic ring.
Round 1: 1 ch, 6 dc into the centre of the ring.
Round 2: 2 dc into each st (12 sts).
Round 3: (1 dc, dc2inc) 6 times (18 sts).
Round 4: (2 dc, dc2inc) 6 times (24 sts).
Round 5: (3 dc, dc2inc) 6 times (30 sts).
Round 6: (4 dc, dc2inc) 6 times (36 sts).
Round 7: (5 dc, dc2inc) 6 times (42 sts).
Round 8: (6 dc, dc2inc) 6 times (48 sts).
Round 9: (7 dc, dc2inc) 6 times (54 sts).
Rounds 10–14: Work 5 rounds straight.
Round 15: (7 dc, dc2tog) 6 times (48 sts).
Round 16: (6 dc, dc2tog) 6 times (42 sts).
Round 17: (5 dc, dc2tog) 6 times (36 sts).
Round 18: (4 dc, dc2tog) 6 times (30 sts).
Round 19: (3 dc, dc2tog) 6 times (24 sts).
Round 20: (2 dc, dc2tog) 6 times (18 sts).
Stuff firmly with some polyester stuffing.
Round 21: (1 dc, dc2tog) 6 times (12 sts).
Round 22: (Dc2tog) 6 times (6 sts).
Fasten off. Weave in ends.

Making up

Turn each cactus inside out. Weave in all ends at the top of the cactus. Stuff each cactus firmly. Sew the flowers to the top of the tall cacti and the bud onto the small cactus. Using the yarn tails, sew each cactus firmly to the crocheted soil piece and place in the plant pot.

Peruvian Apple

This tall, tree-like cactus is native to South America and the Caribbean. It can be blue-green in colour, which I have indicated using this teal yarn. I have reproduced its knobbly spines using popcorn stitch.

FINISHED SIZE

The cactus is approximately 4in (10cm) tall and 3.5in (9cm) wide.

TENSION

Tension is not essential for this project.

YOU WILL NEED

- Scheepjes Cahlista, 100% cotton (93yd/85m per 50g ball):
  1 ball in 401 Dark Teal (A)
  1 ball in 157 Root Beer (B)
- 4mm (UK8:USG/6) crochet hook
- Polyester stuffing
- Tapestry needle
- Plant pot approximately 3½in (9cm) in diameter

Note

The cactus is worked in spirals using the standard amigurumi technique (see page 126). The knobbly bits are created using popcorn stitch (pop; see page 129).

Cactus

Using 4mm (UK8:USG/6) hook and A, make a magic ring (see page 127).

Round 1: 1 ch, 6 dc into the centre of the ring.

Round 2: 2 dc into each st (12 sts).

Round 3: (1 dc, dc2inc) 6 times (18 sts).

Round 4: (2 dc, dc2inc) 6 times (24 sts).

Round 5: (1 pop, 2 dc, dc2inc) 6 times (30 sts).

Round 6: (4 dc, dc2inc) 6 times (36 sts).

Round 7: (1 pop, 4 dc, dc2inc) 6 times (42 sts).

Round 8: (6 dc, dc2inc) 6 times (48 sts).

Round 9: (1 pop, 7 dc) 6 times (48 sts).

Round 10: Work 1 round straight (48 sts).

Rounds 11–14: Rep rounds 9 and 10 twice.

Round 15: (1 pop, 7 dc) 6 times (48 sts).

Round 16: (6 dc, dc2tog) 6 times (42 sts).

Round 17: (1 pop, 6 dc) 6 times (42 sts).

Round 18: (5 dc, dc2tog) 6 times (36 sts).

Round 19: (1 pop, 5 dc) 6 times (36 sts).

Round 20: (4 dc, dc2tog) 6 times (30 sts).

Round 21: (1 pop, 4 dc) 6 times (30 sts).

Round 22: (3 dc, dc2tog) 6 times (24 sts).

Round 23: (1 pop, 3 dc) 6 times (24 sts).

Round 24: (2 dc, dc2tog) 6 times (18 sts).

Fasten off. Leave a yarn tail.

actual size

Soil

Using 3.5mm (UK9:USE/4) hook and B, make a magic ring (see page 127).

Round 1: 1 ch, 6 dc into the centre of the ring.

Round 2: 2 dc into each st (12 sts).

Round 3: (1 dc, dc2inc) 6 times (18 sts).

Round 4: (2 dc, dc2inc) 6 times (24 sts).

Round 5: (3 dc, dc2inc) 6 times (30 sts).

Round 6: (4 dc, dc2inc) 6 times (36 sts).

Rounds 7–14: Work 8 rounds straight.

Round 15: (4 dc, dc2tog) 6 times (30 sts).

Round 16: (3 dc, dc2tog) 6 times (24 sts).

Round 17: (2 dc, dc2tog) 6 times (18 sts). Stuff firmly with polyester stuffing.

Round 18: (1 dc, dc2tog) 6 times (12 sts).

Round 19: (Dc2tog) 6 times (6 sts). Using a tapestry needle, weave this yarn through the last dc sts of the round and gather hole together. Fasten off and weave in ends.

Making up

Firmly stuff the cactus. Using the tapestry needle and long tail of yarn, sew some small stitches along the last round of crochet and slightly pull them to gather the end together. Using the yarn tail from the cactus, sew the plant firmly to the soil and place in the pot.

Alternatively, instead of crocheting the soil, close the cactus by using the tail of yarn to gather the last stitches together. Poke a cocktail stick through the base of the cactus. Cut some floral foam to fit the pot and insert the cocktail stick into the foam to secure the cactus in the pot. Then fill up the sides with small alpine grit.

Cardon Grande

This cactus can grow up to 10ft (33m) tall. If you want to create it in realistic colours, its spines are actually maroon or dark red. Like the Notocactus project (page 50), the spikes are made with a tinsel or eyelash yarn, so if you like the effect, make them both and display them together.

FINISHED SIZE

The cactus is approximately 3¼in (8cm) tall and 2½in (6cm) wide.

YOU WILL NEED

- Robin Double Knit, 100% acrylic (328yd/300m per 100g ball):
  1 ball in 045 Forest (A)
  Small amount in 143 Mink (B)
- Rico Design Creative Bubble, 100% polyester (98yd/90m 50g ball):
  1 ball in 002 Yellow (C)
- 3.5mm (UK9:USE/4) crochet hook
- Tapestry needle
- Polyester stuffing
- Plant pot approximately 2½in (6cm) in diameter

TENSION

Tension is not essential for this project.

Note

The cactus is worked in rows. The rib is created by working into the back loop of each stitch (see page 131).

Cactus

Row 1: Using 3.5mm (UK9:USE/4) hook and A, ch 17 sts.

Row 2 WS: 1 htr in 3rd ch from hook, htr into each ch to end, turn (15 sts).

Row 3: Ch 2, htr tbl into each st to end, turn (15 sts).

Row 3 forms the pattern.

Work a further 12 rows.

With RS together, crochet the first and last rows together:

Next row: Ch 1, sl st in every st.

Fasten off and leave a long yarn tail.

Spikes

Using 3.5mm (UK9:USE/4) hook and C, with RS facing, crochet along the ridges created by the htr. Attach the yarn using a sl st and double crochet in each stitch. Fasten off. You will complete 7 rows of spikes.

Soil

Using 3.5mm (UK9:USE/4) hook and B, make a magic ring (see page 127).

Round 1: 1 ch, 6 dc into the centre of the ring.

Round 2: 2 dc into each st (12 sts).

Round 3: (1 dc, dc2inc) 6 times (18 sts).

Round 4: (2 dc, dc2inc) 6 times (24 sts).

Round 5: 1 dc in each st tbl (24 sts).

Rounds 6–12: Work 7 rounds straight.

Round 13: (2 dc, dc2tog) 6 times (18 sts). Stuff firmly with polyester stuffing.

Round 14: (1 dc, dc2tog) 6 times (12 sts).

Round 15: (Dc2tog) 6 times (6 sts).

Using a tapestry needle, weave this yarn through the last dc sts of the round and gather hole together. Fasten off and weave in ends.

actual size

Making up

Weave in all ends. Make small running stitches along both side seams, and then gather the ends together. Firmly stuff the cactus. Using the yarn tail from the cactus, sew the plant firmly to the soil and place in the pot. Alternatively, cut some floral foam to fit the pot.

Poke a cocktail stick through the base of the cactus, then insert the cocktail stick into the foam to secure the cactus in the pot. Then fill up the sides with small alpine grit. You can crochet a pot for the cactus using one of the patterns on page 138.

Bishop's Cap

This small cactus can grow to around 8in (20cm) in diameter. It has no spines, but does have scales. In nature it has between three and seven ribbed segments; my version is made by sewing together six separate segments.

FINISHED SIZE

The cactus is approximately 3¼in (8cm) in diameter.

TENSION

Tension is not essential for this project.

YOU WILL NEED

- Scheepjes Merino Soft, 50% wool, 25% microfibre, 25% acrylic (115yd/105m per 50g ball): 1 ball in 626 Kahlo
- 3.5mm (UK9:USE/4) crochet hook
- Polyester stuffing
- Tapestry needle
- Cocktail stick
- Floral foam to fit pot
- Small alpine grit
- Plant pot approximately 2½in (6cm) in diameter

Note

The cactus is worked in spirals using the standard amigurumi technique (see page 126). Place a marker at the beginning of each round so you know where you are in the pattern.

Cactus segments (make 6)

Using 3.5mm (UK9:USE/4) hook, make a magic ring (see page 127).

Round 1: 1 ch, 6 dc into the centre of the ring.

Round 2: 2 dc into each st (12 sts).

Round 3: (1 dc, dc2inc) 6 times (18 sts).

Round 4: (2 dc, dc2inc) 6 times (24 sts).

Round 5: (3 dc, dc2inc) 6 times (30 sts).

Round 6: (4 dc, dc2inc) 6 times (36 sts).

Round 7: Work 1 round straight.

Fasten off. Leave a yarn tail of approximately 20in (50cm) to create the segments.

Tip

Don't forget that you can make much larger versions of these makes by increasing the weight and thickness of your yarn and increasing your hook size. You could also add a flower, such as the one from the Ball Cactus on page 86.

actual size

Making up

To make each segment, fold the circle in half to create a semicircle, and using the yarn end, 1 ch, sl st two sides of the semicircles together. When you have reached halfway, stuff with a little polyester stuffing. Complete joining both sides of the semicircles together.

When you have made six segments, with your tapestry needle and a strand of yarn A, sew all six pieces together with some small stitches at the top, then attach the bottom of each segment with some small stitches.

Cut some floral foam to fit the pot. Poke a cocktail stick through the base of the cactus, then insert the cocktail stick into the foam to secure the cactus in the pot. Then fill up the sides with small alpine grit.

Alternatively, crochet some soil using the pattern for the appropriate sized pot on page 137. Using one of the yarn tails from the cactus, sew the plant firmly to the soil and place in the pot. Weave in the other yarn ends. You could also crochet a pot for the cactus using one of the patterns on page 138.

Ball Cactus

This small cactus, native to Brazil, grows to about 6in (15cm) in diameter. It produces spectacular magenta or purple flowers, which I have reproduced in crocheted form in this project.

FINISHED SIZE

The cactus is approximately 3½in (9cm) in diameter.

YOU WILL NEED

- Stylecraft Special DK, 100% acrylic (323yd/295m per 100g ball):
  1 ball in 1826 Kelly Green (A)
  Small amounts in 1054 Walnut (B) and 1083 Pomegranate (C)
- 3.5mm (UK9:USE/4) crochet hook
- Polyester stuffing
- Tapestry needle
- Plant pot approximately 3½in (9cm) in diameter

TENSION

Tension is not essential for this project.

Note

The cactus is worked in rows. The rib is created by working into the back loop of each stitch (see page 131). The soil is worked in spiral rounds using the amigurumi technique (see page 126). Place a marker at the beginning of each round so you know where you are in the pattern.

Large cactus

Row 1: Using 3.5mm (UK9:USE/4) hook and A, ch 13 sts.
Row 2 WS: 1 dc in 2nd ch from hook, dc into each ch to end, turn (12 sts).
Row 3: Ch 1, dc tbl into each st to end, turn (12 sts).
Row 3 forms the pattern.
Work a further 26 rows.
With RS together, crochet the first and last rows together:
Next row: Ch 1, sl st in every st.
Fasten off and leave a long yarn tail.

Small cactus (make 2)

Row 1: Using 3.5mm (UK9:USE/4) hook and A, ch 7 sts.
Row 2 WS: 1 dc in 2nd ch from hook, dc into each ch to end, turn (6 sts).
Row 3: Ch 1, dc tbl into each st to end, turn (6 sts).
Row 3 forms the pattern. Work a further 14 rows.
With RS together, crochet the first and last rows together:
Next row: Ch 1, sl st in every st.
Fasten off and leave a long yarn tail.

Flower (make 2)

Using 3.5mm (UK9:USE/4) hook and C, make a magic ring (see page 127).
Round 1: 1 ch, 5 dc into the centre of the ring, join with a sl st.
Round 2: (Ch 2, 2 tr, 2 ch, sl st), in first st, *sl st in next st, 2 ch, 2 tr, 2 ch, sl st in same st; rep from * 3 times.
Fasten off. Leave a yarn tail.

Soil

Using 3.5mm (UK9:USE/4) hook and B, make a magic ring (see page 127).
Round 1: 1 ch, 6 dc into the centre of the ring.
Round 2: 2 dc into each st (12 sts).
Round 3: (1 dc, dc2inc) 6 times (18 sts).
Round 4: (2 dc, dc2inc) 6 times (24 sts).
Round 5: (3 dc, dc2inc) 6 times (30 sts).
Round 6: (4 dc, dc2inc) 6 times (36 sts).
Round 7: (5 dc, dc2inc) 6 times (42 sts).
Round 8: (6 dc, dc2inc) 6 times (48 sts).

Rounds 9–12: Work 4 rounds straight.
Round 13: (6 dc, dc2tog) 6 times (42 sts).
Round 14: (5 dc, dc2tog) 6 times (36 sts).
Round 15: (4 dc, dc2tog) 6 times (30 sts).
Round 16: (3 dc, dc2tog) 6 times (24 sts).
Round 17: (2 dc, dc2tog) 6 times (18 sts).
Stuff firmly with some polyester stuffing.
Round 18: (1 dc, dc2tog) 6 times (12 sts).
Round 19: (Dc2tog) 6 times (6 sts).
Fasten off. Weave in ends.

actual siz

Making up

With your tapestry needle and yarn A, sew small stitches along both side seams. Gather the ends together, firmly stuff the cacti and join. Sew a flower to the top of the large cactus, pull the needle down through the stuffing and secure to the base of the cactus so that it creates a small indent on the top. Do the same for one of the small cactus. Sew the other small cactus to the top of the large cactus. Using the yarn tail, sew firmly to the crocheted soil. Place in a plant pot, or you could use a teacup or sugar bowl for display.

Mexican Snowball

As its name suggests, this succulent is native to Mexico.
It is considered to be easy to care for and will grow in clusters
or colonies. It is notable for its elegant colour, a cool mint or
grey-green, which I have tried to reproduce in yarn form.

FINISHED SIZE

The succulent is approximately 4in
(10cm) in diameter.

TENSION

Tension is not essential for
this project.

YOU WILL NEED

- Rico Design Creative Melange
  Lace, 95% cotton, 5% polyester
  (284yd/260m per 50g ball):
  1 ball in 004 Aqua Mix
- 2.75mm (UK12:USC/2) crochet hook
- Polyester stuffing
- Tapestry needle
- Floristry wire
- Floral foam to fit pot
- Small alpine grit
- Plant pot approximately 3½in (9cm)
  in diameter

Note

The succulent leaves are
worked in spirals using the standard
amigurumi technique (see page 126).
Place a marker at the beginning of each
round so you know where you are in
the pattern. You can then sew
them together to create the
whole plant.

Large leaf
(make 10)

Using 2.75mm (UK12:USC/2) hook, make a magic ring (see page 127).

Round 1: 1 ch, 4 dc into the centre of the ring.

Round 2: 1 dc in each st (4 sts).

Round 3: 2 dc in each st (8 sts).

Round 4: (1 dc, dc2inc) 4 times (12 sts).

Round 5: (2 dc, dc2inc) 4 times (16 sts).

Round 6: (3 dc, dc2inc) 4 times (20 sts).

Rounds 7–8: Work 2 rounds straight.

Round 9: (8 dc, dc2tog) twice (18 sts).

Round 10: (7 dc, dc2tog) twice (16 sts).

Round 11: (6 dc, dc2tog) twice (14 sts).

Round 12: (5 dc, dc2tog) twice (12 sts).

Round 13: (4 dc, dc2tog) twice (10 sts).

Round 14: (3 dc, dc2tog) twice (8 sts).

Round 15: Work 1 round straight.

Fasten off. Leave a yarn tail.

actual size

Small leaf
(make 3)

Using 2.75mm (UK12:USC/2) hook, make a magic ring (see page 127).
Round 1: 1 ch, 4 dc into the centre of the ring.
Round 2: 1 dc in each st (4 sts).
Round 3: 2 dc in each st (8 sts).
Round 4: (1 dc, dc2inc) 4 times (12 sts).
Round 5: (2 dc, dc2inc) 4 times (16 sts).
Rounds 6–7: Work 2 rounds straight.
Round 8: (6 dc, dc2tog) twice (14 sts).
Round 9: (5 dc, dc2tog) twice (12 sts).
Round 10: (4 dc, dc2tog) twice (10 sts).
Round 11: (3 dc, dc2tog) twice (8 sts).
Round 12: (2 dc, dc2tog) twice (6 sts).
Fasten off. Leave a yarn tail.

Centre

Using 2.75mm (UK12:USC/2) hook, make a magic ring (see page 127).
Round 1: 1 ch, 6 dc into the centre of the ring.
Round 2: 2 dc into each st (12 sts).
Round 3: (1 dc, dc2inc) 6 times (18 sts).
Rounds 4–5: Work 2 rounds straight.
Round 6: (1 dc, dc2tog) 6 times (12 sts).
Round 7: (Dc2tog) 6 times (6 sts).
Fasten off. Stuff with a small amount of polyester stuffing. Leave a yarn tail.

Making up

Fold each leaf in half and press it flat with your hand. Arrange five large leaves to form a star shape. Using the tail of yarn, sew the end rows together to form a flat star. Do this twice to form two flat stars of five large leaves each. Sew one star of leaves on top of the other, making sure the leaves overlap. Then space the three small leaves equally to form a trefoil. Sew these together and then sew them on top of your large leaves. Finally, sew the small centre ball right in the middle.

Take some floristry wire, fold it in half and thread it through the centre underside of the succulent. Cut some floral foam to fit the pot and insert the wire into the foam to secure the plant in the pot. Fill the pot with some small alpine grit.

String of Pearls

This unusual succulent is considered to be easy to grow indoors and looks stunning with its long, trailing stems cascading from a hanging basket or pot holder. I used the bobble technique to recreate its spherical, bead-like leaves.

FINISHED SIZE

The longest strands are approximately 8in (20cm) long.

YOU WILL NEED

- Scheepjes Merino Soft, 50% wool, 25% microfibre, 25% acrylic (115yd/105m per 50g ball): 1 ball in 629 Constable (A) Small amount in 607 Braque (B)
- 3.5mm (UK9:USE/4) crochet hook
- Polyester stuffing
- Tapestry needle
- Plant pot approximately 3¼in (8cm) in diameter

TENSION

Tension is not essential for this project.

Note

The leaves are created using bobble stitch (see page 130). If you want to create longer strands, simply repeat the bobble count more.

Large strand
(make 4)

Use 3.5mm (UK9:USE/4) hook and A.

Row 1: Ch 3, make bobble in 1st ch, *7 ch, make bobble in 3rd ch from hook; rep from * 7 times, 5 ch (9 bobbles). Fasten off and leave a tail of yarn.

Small strand
(make 5)

Use 3.5mm (UK9:USE/4) hook and A.

Row 1: Ch 3, make bobble in 1st ch, *7 ch, make bobble in 3rd ch from hook; rep from * twice, 5 ch (4 bobbles). Fasten off and leave a tail of yarn.

Medium strand
(make 3)

Use 3.5mm (UK9:USE/4) hook and A.

Row 1: Ch 3, make bobble in 1st ch, *7 ch, make bobble in 3rd ch from hook; rep from * 4 times, 5 ch (6 bobbles). Fasten off and leave a tail of yarn.

actual size

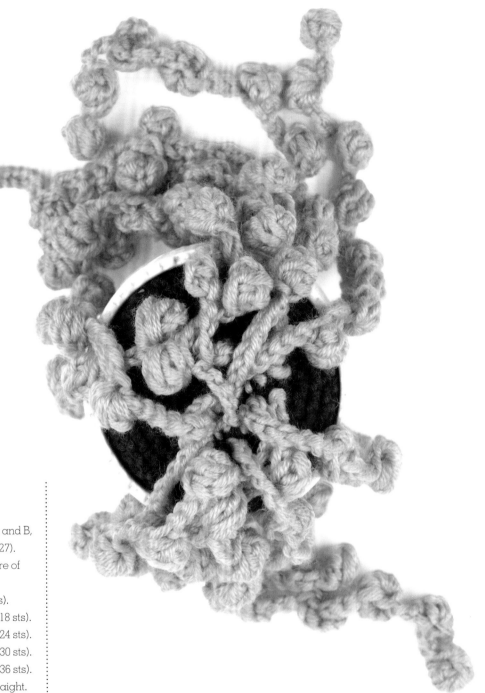

Soil for pot

Using 3.5mm (UK9:USE/4) hook and B, make a magic ring (see page 127).

Round 1: 1 ch, 6 dc into the centre of the ring.

Round 2: 2 dc into each st (12 sts).

Round 3: (1 dc, dc2inc) 6 times (18 sts).

Round 4: (2 dc, dc2inc) 6 times (24 sts).

Round 5: (3 dc, dc2inc) 6 times (30 sts).

Round 6: (4 dc, dc2inc) 6 times (36 sts).

Rounds 7–11: Work 5 rounds straight.

Round 12: (4 dc, dc2tog) 6 times (30 sts).

Round 13: (3 dc, dc2tog) 6 times (24 sts).

Round 14: (2 dc, dc2tog) 6 times (18 sts). Stuff firmly with some polyester stuffing.

Round 15: (1 dc, dc2tog) 6 times (12 sts).

Round 16: (Dc2tog) 6 times (6 sts). Fasten off. Weave in ends.

Making up

Using the long tail of yarn, sew each end of the strands to the centre of the soil, place in the pot, and drape the long strings over the edge of the pot.

Blue Waves

This succulent grows to about 12in (30cm) in diameter and is notable for its pretty blue-green colour and slightly frilly, pointed leaves. Unlike the other Echeveria projects in this book (Moulded Wax Agave, page 30 and Romeo Wax Agave, page 58) this plant is crocheted in one piece.

FINISHED SIZE

The succulent is approximately 2¾in (7cm) in diameter.

TENSION

Tension is not essential for this project.

YOU WILL NEED

- Scheepjes Catona, 100% cotton (137yd/125m per 50g ball): 1 ball in 402 Silver Green
- 3.5mm (UK9:USE/4) crochet hook
- Floristry wire
- Floral foam to fit pot
- Small alpine grit
- Plant pot approximately 3½in (9cm) in diameter

Note

The succulent is worked in rounds. Start in the centre and then build the round of leaves below.

Succulent

Using 3.5mm (UK9:USE/4) hook, make a magic ring (see page 127).

Round 1: 1 ch, 6 dc into the centre of the ring, join with a sl st.

Round 2: (Ch 2, sl st in next st), *sl st into next st, 2 ch, sl st in next st; rep from * (3 loops).

Round 3: *Sl st in ch sp, (2 ch, 3 tr, 2 ch, 1 sl st) in ch sp; rep from * twice (3 leaves).

Round 4: Folding leaves forward and working into the back of each leaf, *4 ch, 1 sl st in base of one tr at the centre of next leaf; rep from * twice (3 loops).

Round 5: *Sl st in ch sp, (2 ch, 3 tr, 2 ch, 1 sl st in first ch, 3 tr, 2 ch 1 sl st) in ch sp; rep from * twice (3 leaves).

Round 6: Folding leaves forward and working into the back of each leaf, *3 ch, 1 sl st in base of one tr at the centre of next leaf, 3 ch, 1 sl st in next sl st between the next leaf of previous row; rep from * twice (6 loops).

Round 7: *Sl st in ch sp, (2 ch, 2 tr, 1 dtr, 2 ch, 1 sl st in first ch, 1 dtr, 2 tr, 2 ch, 1 sl st) in ch sp; rep from * 5 times (6 leaves).

Round 8: Folding leaves forward and working into the back of each leaf, *4 ch, 1 sl st in base of one dtr at the centre of next leaf; rep from * 5 times (6 loops).

Round 9: *Sl st in ch sp, (2 ch, 1 tr, 2 dtr, 2 ch, 1 sl st in first ch, 2 dtr, 1 tr, 2 ch, 1 sl st) in ch sp; rep from * 5 times (6 leaves).

Fasten off. Weave in ends.

Tip

Try creating new textures by combining two yarns together. This will create a natural variegation often found in nature.

actual size

Making up

Cut some floral foam to fit the pot. Take some floristry wire, fold it in half, and thread it through the centre underside of the succulent. Insert the wire into the foam to secure the plant in the pot. Fill the pot with small alpine grit.

Pig's Ear

This pretty succulent is native to South Africa and comes in a range of colours in the wild. Often the edges of the leaves are tinged with red. I have recreated this by crocheting a line of slip stitches along the top edge of the large leaves.

FINISHED SIZE

The large leaves are approximately 3¼in (8cm) long and 2½in (6cm) wide.

YOU WILL NEED

- Stylecraft Linen Drape, 70% viscose, 30% linen (202yd/185m per 100g ball):
  1 ball in 3904 River (A)
  Small amount in 3908 Cranberry (B)
- 3.5mm (UK9:USE/4) crochet hook
- Tapestry needle
- Cocktail sticks
- Floral foam to fit pot
- Plant pot approximately 2¾in (7cm) in diameter

TENSION

Tension is not essential for this project.

Note

The cactus is worked in spirals using the standard amigurumi technique (see page 126). Place a marker at the beginning of each round so you know where you are in the pattern.

Large leaf (make 4)

Using 3.5mm (UK9:USE/4) hook and A, make a magic ring (see page 127).

Round 1: 1 ch, 5 dc into the centre of the ring.

Round 2: 2 dc into each st (10 sts).

Round 3: (4 dc, dc2inc) rep (12 sts).

Round 4: (5 dc, dc2inc) rep (14 sts).

Round 5: (6 dc, dc2inc) rep (16 sts).

Round 6: (7 dc, dc2inc) rep (18 sts).

Round 7: (8 dc, dc2inc) rep (20 sts).

Round 8: (9 dc, dc2inc) rep (22 sts).

Rounds 9–11: Work 3 rounds straight.

Round 12: (9 dc, dc2tog) rep (20 sts).

Round 13: Work 1 round straight (20 sts).

Round 14: (8 dc, dc2tog) rep (18 sts).

Round 15: Work 1 round straight (18 sts).

Round 16: (7 dc, dc2tog) rep (16 sts).

Round 17: Work 1 round straight (16 sts).

Round 18: (6 dc, dc2tog) rep (14 sts).

Round 19: (5 dc, dc2tog) rep (12 sts).

Round 20: (4 dc, dc2tog) rep (10 sts).

Fasten off. Leave a yarn tail to sew to other leaves.

Small leaf (make 2)

Using 3.5mm (UK9:USE/4) hook and A, make a magic ring (see page 127).

Round 1: 1 ch, 5 dc into the centre of the ring.

Round 2: 2 dc into each st (10 sts).

Round 3: (4 dc, dc2inc) rep (12 sts).

Round 4: (5 dc, dc2inc) rep (14 sts).

Rounds 5–6: Work 2 rounds straight.

Round 7: (5 dc, dc2tog) rep (12 sts).

Round 8: Work 1 round straight (12 sts).

Round 9: (4 dc, dc2tog) rep (10 sts).

Round 10: (3 dc, dc2tog) rep (8 sts).

Fasten off. Leave a yarn tail to sew to other leaves.

actual size

Making up

Flatten each leaf with the palm of your hand. On each large leaf, crochet a line of slip stitches along the top of each leaf using yarn B. As a guide, attach the yarn on round 6 and then sl st along the top of the leaf until you reach round 6 on the other side. Fasten off and weave in ends.

Sew the bases of the two small leaves together, ensuring they are at an angle. Then sew two large leaves on each side of the two small leaves. Try to angle the leaves so that they look natural.

Place a cocktail stick through the base of a small leaf and on both outer large leaves. Place a piece of floral foam in the base of your pot. Then insert the cocktail sticks into the foam to secure the plant in the pot.

Old Lady Cactus

This succulent, native to Mexico, is covered in white down and white spines. By using two strands of yarn together – a basic cotton and a fluffy eyelash yarn – I was able to recreate this fabulous effect in crocheted form. This cactus looks even better if you turn the crochet inside out and have the normal wrong side of the material showing.

FINISHED SIZE

The cactus is approximately 3½in (9cm) in diameter.

YOU WILL NEED

- Stylecraft Cotton Classique, 100% cotton (101yd/92m per 50g ball): 1 ball in 3097 Leaf (A)
- Stylecraft Eskimo Double Knitting, 100% polyester (98yd/90m per 50g ball): 1 ball in 5006 Winter White (B)
- 4mm (UK8:USG/6) crochet hook
- Polyester stuffing
- Tapestry needle
- Floristry wire
- Floral foam to fit pot
- Plant pot approximately 2½in (6cm) in diameter

TENSION

Tension is not essential for this project.

Note

The cactus is worked in spirals using the standard amigurumi technique (see page 126). Place a marker at the beginning of each round so you know where you are in the pattern. Use both strands of the yarn held together to create the effect. Turn the finished crochet wrong side out before you stuff it.

Cactus

Using 4mm (UK8:USG/6) hook and 1 strand of A and 1 strand of B held together, make a magic ring (see page 127).

Round 1: 1 ch, 6 dc into the centre of the ring.

Round 2: 2 dc into each st (12 sts).

Round 3: (1 dc, dc2inc) 6 times (18 sts).

Round 4: (2 dc, dc2inc) 6 times (24 sts).

Round 5: (3 dc, dc2inc) 6 times (30 sts).

Rounds 6–9: Work 4 rounds straight.

Round 10: (3 dc, dc2tog) 6 times (24 sts).

Round 11: (2 dc, dc2tog) 6 times (18 sts). Stuff firmly with some polyester stuffing.

Round 12: (1 dc, dc2tog) 6 times (12 sts).

Round 13: (Dc2tog) 6 times (6 sts). Fasten off. Weave in ends.

Tip

Your cactus creations make wonderful presents. If you have a sewing addict among your friends and family, why not give them one to use as a pincushion?

actual size

Making up

Take some floristry wire, fold it in half and thread it through the centre underside of the succulent. Cut some floral foam to fit the pot. Insert the wire into the foam to secure the plant in the pot. Alternatively you could crochet a pot for the cactus using one of the patterns on page 138.

Devil's Tongue

This cactus, native to Mexico, is usually globe-shaped or spherical. Its ferocious-looking spines, from where it derives its common name, are usually red. I have recreated the spiky effect by using tinsel yarn.

FINISHED SIZE

The cactus is approximately 4in (10cm) in diameter.

TENSION

Tension is not essential for this project.

YOU WILL NEED

- Robin Double Knit, 100% acrylic (328yd/300m per 100g ball): 1 ball in 045 Forest (A)
- Rico Design Creative Bubble, 100% polyester (98yd/90m per 50g ball): 1 ball in 018 Dark Red (B)
- 3.5mm (UK9:USE/4) crochet hook
- Polyester stuffing
- Tapestry needle
- Floristry wire
- Floral foam to fit pot
- Small alpine grit
- Plant pot approximately 2½in (6cm) in diameter

Note

The cactus is worked in spirals using the standard amigurumi technique (see page 126). Place a marker at the beginning of each round so you know where you are in the pattern. You crochet each segment in yarn A, then embroider the spines on afterwards in yarn B.

Cactus segments
(make 8)

Using 3.5mm (UK9:USE/4) hook and A,
make a magic ring (see page 127).

Round 1: 1 ch, 6 dc into the centre
of the ring.

Round 2: 2 dc into each st (12 sts).

Round 3: (1 dc, dc2inc) 6 times (18 sts).

Round 4: (2 dc, dc2inc) 6 times (24 sts).

Round 5: (3 dc, dc2inc) 6 times (30 sts).

Round 6: (4 dc, dc2inc) 6 times (36 sts).

Fasten off. Leave a long yarn tail to
create the segments.

Tip

*Tinsel yarn can sometimes be quite
difficult to use. Always crochet in good
light and don't worry too much if you
make a mistake – it'll just look even
more natural!*

actual size

Making up

To make each segment, fold the circle in half to create a semicircle, and using the yarn tail, 1 ch, sl st two sides of the semicircles together. When you are three-quarters of the way along, remove the hook. Take a length of B and your tapestry needle and over-stitch on the seam. Stitch 3 times in the same place to create each spine. As a guide, stitch about 5 sets of spines on each segment, approximately 3 sl sts apart. Then stuff the segment with a little polyester stuffing. Complete joining both sides of the semicircles together. Fasten off and weave in ends.

When you have made eight segments, attach all eight with some small sewn stitches at the top and some small stitches at the bottom.

Insert some floristry wire through the base of the cactus. Cut some floral foam to fit the pot and insert the wire into the foam to secure the cactus in the pot. Then fill up the sides with small alpine grit.

Holiday Cactus

Native to Brazil, this plant is considered relatively easy to grow indoors. It derives its common name from the fact that it flowers in midwinter, adding some much-welcome vibrant colour to the season.

FINISHED SIZE

The longest strands are approximately 10in (25cm) long.

TENSION

Tension is not essential for this project.

YOU WILL NEED

- ◆ Robin Double Knit, 100% acrylic (328yd/300m per 100g ball):
  1 ball in 045 Forest (A)
  1 ball in 064 Fiesta (B)
- ◆ 3.5mm (UK9:USE/4) crochet hook
- ◆ Tapestry needle
- ◆ Fork (to make pompoms)
- ◆ Floristry wire
- ◆ Floral foam to fit pot
- ◆ Square of brown felt 6 x 6in (15 x 15cm)
- ◆ Craft glue
- ◆ Plant pot approximately 4in (10cm) in diameter

Large strand
(make 3)

Using 3.5mm (UK9:USE/4) hook and A, ch 35.

Row 1: 1 tr in third ch, 1 tr in next two ch sts, 2 ch, sl st into ch at base of last tr, *sl st in next 3 ch sts, 2 ch, 1 tr in same st as last sl st, 1 tr in next two ch sts, 2 ch, sl st into ch at base of tr, rep from * 5 times, 1 ch, (now turn and work down the other side of the foundation ch), 1 sl st in first ch, 2 ch, 1 tr in same st as last sl st, 1 tr in next two ch sts, 2 ch, sl st into ch at base of tr, *sl st in next 3 ch sts, 2 ch, 1 tr in same st as last sl st, 1 tr in next two ch sts, 2 ch, sl st into ch at base of tr; rep from * 5 times (7 leaves). Fasten off and leave a long tail of yarn.

Medium strand (make 5)

Using 3.5mm hook (UK9:USE/4) and A, ch 25.

Row 1: 1 tr in third ch, 1 tr in next two ch sts, 2 ch, sl st into ch at base of last tr, *sl st in next 3 ch sts, 2 ch, 1 tr in same st as last sl st, 1 tr in next two ch sts, 2 ch, sl st into ch at base of tr, rep from * 3 times, 1 ch, (now turn and work down the other side of the foundation ch), 1 sl st in first ch, 2 ch, 1 tr in same st as last sl st, 1 tr in next two ch sts, 2 ch, sl st into ch at base of tr, *sl st in next 3 ch sts, 2 ch, 1 tr in same st as last sl st, 1 tr in next two ch sts, 2 ch, sl st into ch at base of tr; rep from * 3 times (5 leaves). Fasten off and leave a long tail of yarn.

Flowers (make up to 10)

Using yarn B, use the fork technique (see page 135) to make a thin pompom by winding the yarn over the end of a fork about 12 times. Sew the pompom firmly to each end of the strands where you have left a tail of yarn.

actual size

Small strand (make 2)

Using 3.5mm (UK9:USE/4) hook and A, ch 20.

Row 1: 1 tr in third ch, 1 tr in next two ch sts, 2 ch, sl st into ch at base of last tr, *sl st in next 3 ch sts, 2 ch, 1 tr in same st as last sl st, 1 tr in next two ch sts, 2 ch, sl st into ch at base of tr, rep from * twice, 1 ch, (now turn and work down the other side of the foundation ch), 1 sl st in first ch, 2 ch, 1 tr in same st as last sl st, 1 tr in next two ch sts, 2 ch, sl st into ch at base of tr, *sl st in next 3 ch sts, 2 ch, 1 tr in same st as last sl st, 1 tr in next two ch sts, 2 ch, sl st into ch at base of tr; rep from * twice (4 leaves). Fasten off and leave a long tail of yarn.

Making up

Weave a length of floristry wire through the middle of each strand of leaves on the wrong side, leaving some sticking out the end. Cut a piece of floral foam to fit your pot. Fold a piece of brown felt over the foam so that it smoothly covers the top to form soil. Using craft glue, stick the felt to the sides of the foam. Place the felt-covered foam into your pot, then poke the floristry wire at the ends of the strands into it. Manipulate the wire to create a natural plant shape.

Getting started

You won't need any traditional gardening equipment to make these horticulture specimens spring to life. Just gather together some easy-to-find craft supplies and watch your succulents collection grow.

CROCHET HOOKS

Crochet hooks come in a range of materials and sizes. Most of the projects in this book are fairly small-scale, so I use hooks ranging from 2.75mm (UK–:USC/2) to 4mm (UK8:USG/6). For these sizes I like to use an ergonomic metal-pointed crochet hook. Larger hooks, such as 8mm (UK0:USL/11) or 9mm (UK00:USM–N/13), are often made in plastic or wood.

YARN

The key issue with making cacti and succulents is to find a yarn that replicates the colour and textures of the plants.

I had so much fun using tinsel or eyelash yarns to create the look of cactus spines, such as with the Notocactus, Cardon Grande and Old Lady Cactus (see pages 50, 78 and 106). Get creative and combine a base colour in a cheap acrylic and then go to town with your spiky fashion yarns. Anyone who sees your creations will feel compelled to touch them just to see if they are real.

You certainly don't have to buy special balls of yarn for these projects. Nowadays some yarn producers sell 10g balls that are perfect for small projects like these. Alternatively, you could use up some scraps and leftovers from other projects.

POLYESTER STUFFING

I have used Minicraft Supersoft toy stuffing to stuff the cacti and succulents. This material complies with BS145, BN5852 and EN71 standards and is safe for children. Make sure plants are stuffed so that they are firm but not bulging, as this will distort the look of the overall plant.

NEEDLES

You will need a tapestry needle for sewing in yarn ends, sewing project pieces or segments together and adding embroidery details. You will need a fine beading needle for sewing on the beads for the Bunny Ears Cactus (see page 66).

Tip

You can use any yarn you like for these projects. For most of the projects I have used a DK weight yarn with a 3.5mm (UK9:USE/4) hook. But you could create a mini-version using a sock yarn or lace-weight yarn with a 2.5mm (UK12:US–) hook or go gigantic and create a cactus footstool with a super chunky yarn and appropriately large hook. I warn you though – chunky yarns are quite physically demanding to work with. You will feel as if you have done a full workout.

COCKTAIL STICKS

I have used cocktail sticks (you could also use toothpicks or wooden skewers) to help attach the crochet to the pot that the plant sits in. Depending on how tall the cactus is, a cocktail stick or skewer will ensure that the plant does not fall over. My suggestion would be to ensure that the wood does not poke through the stitches when inserted into the inside of the plant, then cut the stick to the right size so that when it is inserted into the pot, the plant is placed just below the rim of the pot.

FLORISTRY WIRE

Thin floristry wire is very useful to create a bend in the leaves of your plant. You can insert the wire through the middle of your crochet piece where it won't be seen. This will then allow you to bend and manipulate your leaves to ensure they look as natural as possible.

Tip

Even experienced crocheters need to check that they have the correct number of stitches or rows. I don't use expensive stitch markers; I just cut a small amount of yarn, about 2in (5cm) long, and place this between the last stitch of one row and the first stitch of the next row. When I have finished, these small strands can easily be pulled out without snagging the stitches. This is especially useful when crocheting in amigurumi style.

FLORAL FOAM

In some of the projects I have used dry floral foam to anchor the crocheted plant to the pot it is placed within, but since I first published this book there has been an increasing awareness of microplastics and how floral foam is not good for the environment. If you already have some floral foam, feel free to use it in these designs. However, the best idea is to crochet soil for your cacti. There are a number of patterns for different size pots on see page 137.

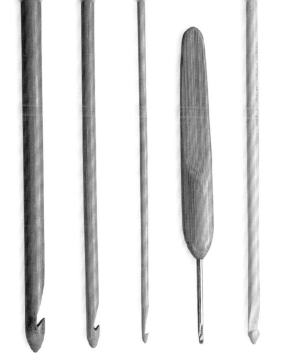

CROCHET HOOK SIZES

UK	Metric	US
14	2mm	–
13	2.25mm	B/1
12	2.5mm	–
–	2.75mm	C/2
11	3mm	–
10	3.25mm	D/3
9	3.5mm	E/4
–	3.75mm	F/5
8	4mm	G/6
7	4.5mm	7
6	5mm	H/8
5	5.5mm	I/9
4	6mm	J/10
3	6.5mm	K/10.5
2	7mm	–
0	8mm	L/11
00	9mm	M–N/13
000	10mm	N–P/15

ABBREVIATIONS

alt	alternate
ch	chain
ch sp	chain space
cm	centimetres
cont	continue
dc	double crochet
dc2inc	double crochet increase by one stitch
dc2tog	double crochet two stitches together (decrease by one stitch)
dc3tog	double crochet three stitches together (decrease by two stitches)
dec	decrease
DK	double knitting
dtr	double treble
g	grams
htr	half treble
in	inch(es)
inc	increase
m	metre(s)
mm	millimetre(s)
rep	repeat
RS	right side
RtrF	raised treble front
sl st	slip stitch
sp	space
st(s)	stitch(es)
tbl	through the back loop
tog	together
tr	treble
yd	yard(s)
yo	yarn over
WS	wrong side

Crochet techniques

In this section you can learn the basic techniques needed for the projects in this book. Some will need a bit of practice, but once you have learnt them you can add texture and decoration to all your crocheted succulents.

HOLDING A HOOK

Hold your hook in either your right or your left hand as you would a pen, in between your index finger and thumb.

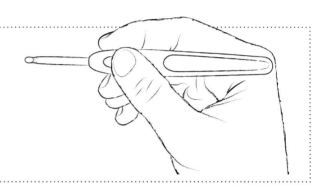

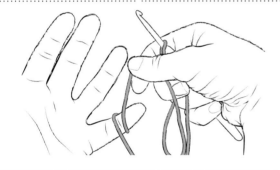

HOLDING YARN

With the hand you are not using to hold the hook, wrap the yarn around your little finger and then drape the yarn over your hand. You can hold the tail of your yarn between the middle finger and your thumb and use your index finger to control the yarn.

MAKING A SLIP KNOT

Make a loop of yarn over two fingers. Pull a second loop through this first loop, pull it up and slip it onto your crochet hook. Pull the knot gently so that it forms a loose knot on the hook.

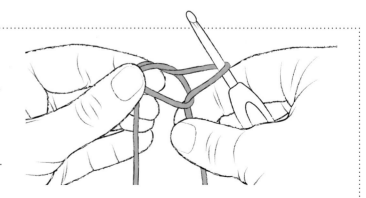

UK AND US DIFFERENCES

Some UK and US terms have different meanings, which can cause confusion, so always check which style the pattern you are using is written in. This will ensure that your crochet develops correctly. There is nothing more frustrating than working on a pattern, then realising it is all wrong and needs to be unravelled.

UK crochet terms	US crochet terms
Double crochet	Single crochet
Half treble	Half double crochet
Treble	Double crochet
Double treble	Triple crochet
Treble treble	Double triple crochet

Note: This book is written in UK crochet terms.

SLIP STITCH (SL ST)

This stitch is ideal for decoration and for attaching two pieces of crochet together.

1   Insert the hook into a stitch, and wrap the yarn over the hook.

2   Draw the loop through the stitch and the loop on the hook. Continue in this way for the required number of slip stitches.

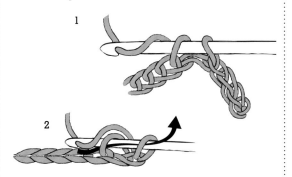

CHAIN STITCH (CH ST)

1   Start with a slip knot on the hook.

2   Wrap the yarn over the hook.

3   Pull the loop through the loop of the slip knot to form one chain stitch.

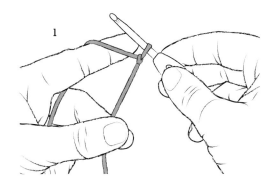

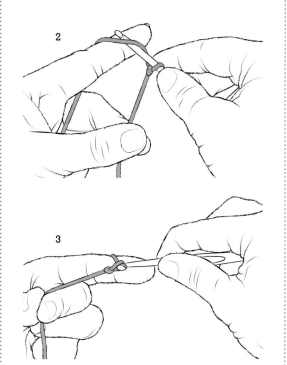

DOUBLE CROCHET (DC)

1 Insert the hook through the stitch, yarn over the hook, and pull through the stitch. There will be two loops on the hook.

2 Wrap the yarn over the hook and pull through both loops on the hook. There will be one loop on the hook.

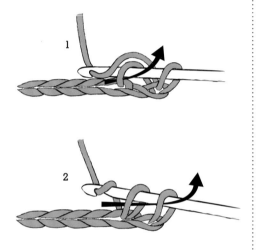

TREBLE CROCHET (TR)

1 Wrap the yarn over the hook, and insert the hook through the stitch. Wrap the yarn over the hook and pull through the stitch.

2 Wrap the yarn over the hook and pull through two loops. There will be two loops on the hook.

3 Wrap the yarn over the hook again and pull through the remaining two loops. There will be one loop left on the hook.

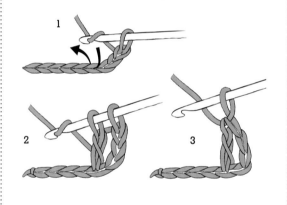

HALF TREBLE (HTR)

1 Wrap the yarn over the hook, insert the hook through the stitch, yarn over the hook and pull through the stitch. There will be three loops on the hook.

2 Wrap the yarn over the hook again and draw through all the loops on the hook. There will be one loop on the hook.

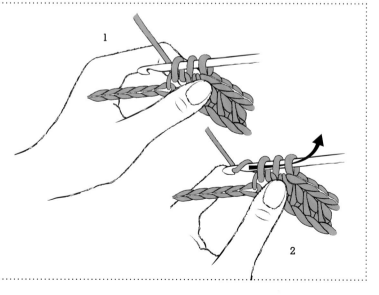

DOUBLE TREBLE (DTR)

1   Wrap the yarn over the hook twice, insert the hook through the stitch, yarn over the hook and pull through the stitch. There will be four loops on the hook.

2   Wrap the yarn over the hook and pull through two loops. There will be three loops on the hook.

3   Wrap the yarn over the hook and pull through two loops. There will be two loops on the hook.

4   Wrap the yarn over and pull through the remaining two loops. There will be one loop on the hook.

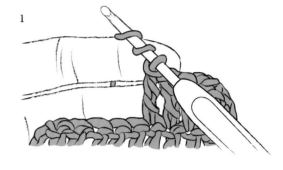

1

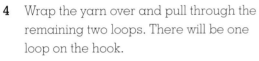

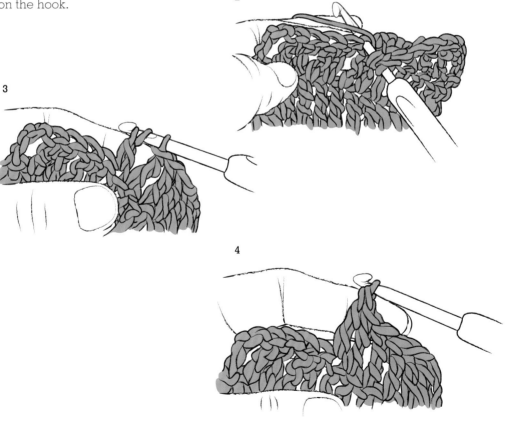

3

2

4

WORKING IN ROWS

When making straight rows, you need to make a turning chain at the beginning of the row for the stitch you are working on. A double crochet row will need one chain at the beginning of the row; this will be indicated in the pattern.

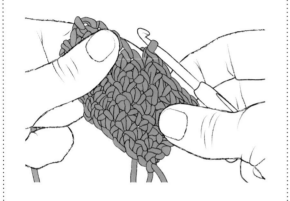

WORKING IN ROUNDS

One wonderful thing about crochet is that you don't always have to work in rows; you can also work in rounds. Many of the patterns in this book are worked in continuous spiral rounds with no slip-stitch joins or turning chains.

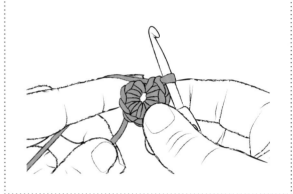

WORKING IN SPIRALS

The majority of the patterns in this book are worked in spiral rounds, beginning with a magic ring. They are worked using the 'amigurumi' crochet technique, which involves crocheting in a continuous spiral with no slip-stitch joins or turning chains. In this way, you can create one seamless cylindrical shape.

In order to know where each row starts, it is advisable to place a marker at the beginning of each row.

MAGIC RING

A clever way to start an amigurumi shape is use a 'magic ring'. This is a neat way of starting a circular piece of crochet while avoiding the unsightly hole that can be left in the centre when you join a ring the normal way. Magic rings are nearly always made with double crochet stitches, as this creates a tight, dense crochet fabric.

1   Start by making a basic slip knot. Pull up the loop and slip this loop onto your crochet hook.

2   Before you tighten the ring, wrap the yarn over the hook (outside the circle) and pull through to make the first chain.

3   Insert the hook into the ring, wrap the yarn over the hook and pull through the ring so there are two loops on the hook.

4   Wrap the yarn over the hook again (outside the circle) and pull through both loops.

5   You have made your first double crochet stitch.

6   Continue to work like this for as many double crochet stitches as are stated in the pattern instructions. Pull the yarn tail to tighten the ring and then continue working in the round as usual.

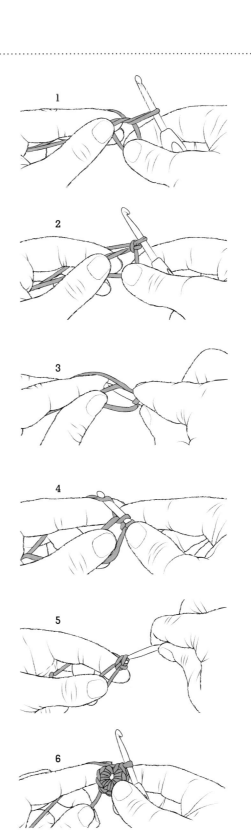

INCREASING (INC)

Work a stitch as normal, then work another into the same stitch of the previous row.

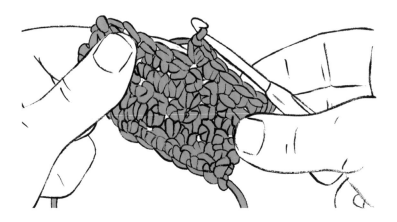

DECREASING (DC2TOG)

1   Insert your hook into the next stitch, pull a loop through, insert your hook into the next stitch, and pull a loop through.

2   Wrap the yarn over the hook and pull the yarn through all three loops.

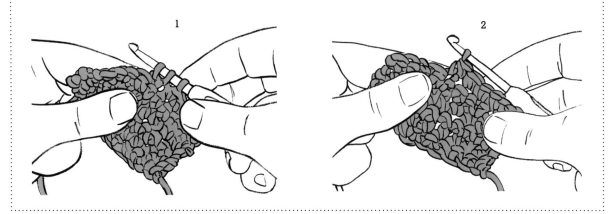

POPCORN (POP)

The Peruvian Apple (see page 74) uses a popcorn stitch. This creates a bobble of yarn that stands proud of the crochet fabric.

1   Work 4tr into the same stitch, leave the loop from the last tr, remove your hook.

2   Remove the hook from the loop and insert it from the back to front through the top of the first tr of the group and pick up the loop left from the last st.

3   Draw the working loop through to the top of the first treble.

4   This will ensure the bobble stands proud of the crochet.

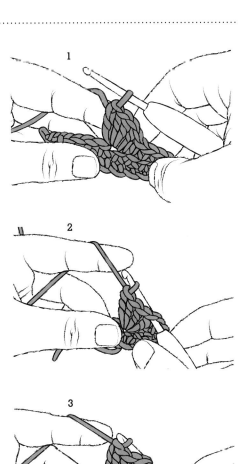

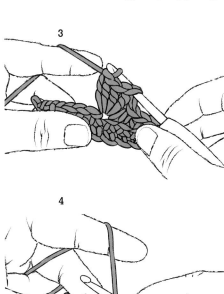

BOBBLE

The String of Pearls pattern (see page 94) creates a bobble by drawing several htr stitches together and then making a sl st in the first ch of the stitch.

1   Work the number of chain stitches specified in the instructions for your pattern.

2   Make 4 htr stitches in the first ch, yarn over.

3   Pull through all five loops on the hook.

4   Sl st in the first ch made at the beginning of the stitch.

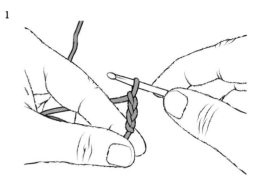

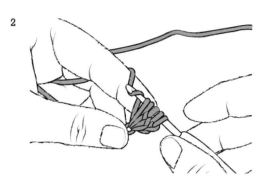

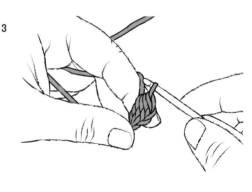

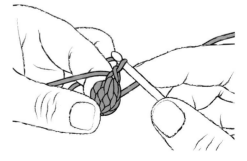

THROUGH THE BACK LOOP (TBL)

Generally, a crochet stitch is made by
slipping the hook under the top two loops
of a stitch. However, you can also create a
different effect by working into the back loop
only of each stitch of one round or row. This
creates a ridge or horizontal bar across the
row. I have used this technique for several
projects in this book, including Mexican
Giant Cardon (page 26), Golden Barrel
(page 46) and Golden Torch (page 70).

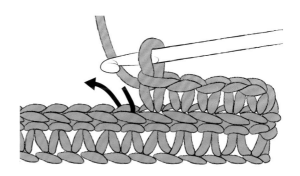

Finishing touches

This section shows you how to make up your finished project so that it is robust and durable, and add embellishments for extra details.

WHIP STITCH

You can use whip stitch to sew two layers of fabric together. Make a knot at the end of your yarn. Bring your needle from the wrong side through to the right side of your fabric, then hold both pieces of your fabric together, wrong sides facing each other. Push your needle from the back piece through to the front piece, and repeat evenly along the edge. There will be a row of small stitches along the edge of your work, joining both pieces together.

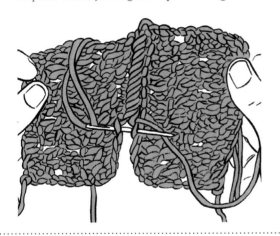

SLIP-STITCH SEAM

Place the pieces of the crochet together with wrong sides facing each other. Insert the hook through both pieces at the beginning of the seam and pull up a loop, then chain one stitch. Work a row of slip stitches by inserting your hook through both sides at the same time.

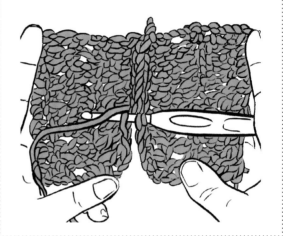

DOUBLE CROCHET SEAMS

Work as for a slip-stitch seam but working double crochet instead of slip stitch. If you work around a corner, work three small stitches into the corners.

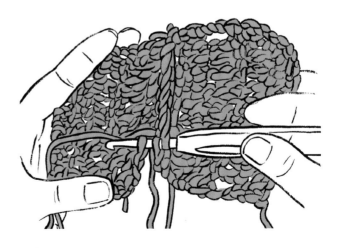

WEAVING IN ENDS

Try to leave about 8in (20cm) of yarn when you fasten off. You may be able to hide the tail in your next row. I always ensure that my ends have been woven backwards and forwards three times.

1 Thread the remaining yarn end onto a tapestry needle and weave in the yarn on the wrong side of the project. Work along the stitches one way, then work back in the opposite direction.

2 Weave the needle behind the first ridge of crochet for at least 2in (5cm). Snip off the end of the yarn close to the fabric of the crochet.

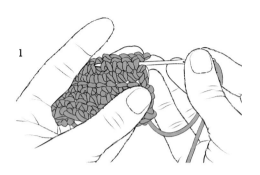

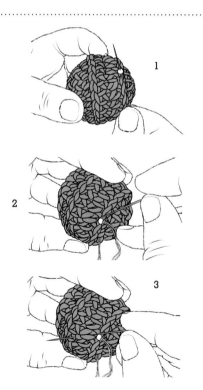

SEWING ON BEADS

The Bunny Ears Cactus (see page 66) features tiny seed beads that are sewn on to the surface of the crochet after your have created each leaf.

1 Take some black cotton sewing thread. Thread onto a very fine needle (size 10/12), knot the end of the thread and then insert up through the inside of the leaf. Start at the top of the leaf and poke your needle out. Place a bead on your needle and make one small stitch.

2 Then push your needle back through.

3 Come out again about two stitches away from your last bead. Try to make your beads seem randomly placed for a natural look.

MAKING A POMPOM WITH A FORK

I love to use a pompom maker. However, the projects in this book (San Pedro, page 34 and Holiday Cactus, page 114) need a much thinner and flatter pompom to replicate the spiky flowers of the cacti. The best way to create these flowers is to use a simple fork.

1   Cut a piece of yarn about 12in (30cm) long and place this on the side of the tines.

2   Wrap the yarn around the fork about 15 times.

3   Knot the piece of yarn that you had along the side of the fork

4   Cut the wool loop on the other side of the fork.

5   Trim your yarn to create a flat pompom.

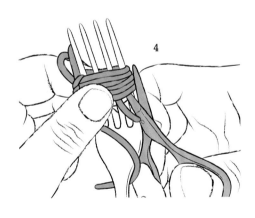

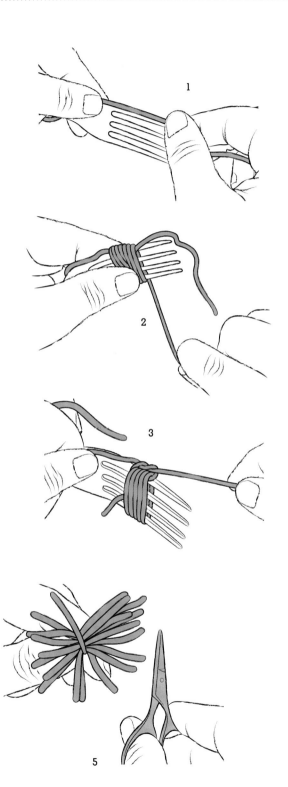

Displaying your succulents

You can use a range of pots to display your succulents: basic terracotta, beautiful glazed pots, and pots that you have crocheted. You can even use an old teacup. The explosion in popularity of succulent plants has made dinky pots readily available, but you could also upcycle an old jam jar or reuse a pot from your garden.

I have secured my plants to their pots in four different ways. Feel free to choose your preferred option for each plant.

In some of the patterns, such as Saguaro (page 22), San Pedro (page 34) and Bunny Ears Cactus (page 66), the soil part of the plant is crocheted as part of the project. The soil part is stuffed, and you can just place the whole crocheted piece into a pot.

The second way is to crochet a separate soil insert: make a small sphere in brown yarn and then fill this with stuffing (see right). Then you can sew your plant to the crochet soil and place the soil within the pot. Patterns for soil inserts for different sizes of pots are given on page 137.

A third option is to place some floral foam in your pot. Then poke some floristry wire or a cocktail stick through the succulent, and insert the other end into the foam to secure your plant in the pot. You can then fill in the gaps with some small alpine grit to give an authentic look.

A fourth option was the technique I used for the Jade Necklace (page 38) and Holiday Cactus (page 114). I glued a piece of brown felt to some floral foam and then wedged this into the pot so that it was secure. I then poked the wires that were in the centre of the long stalks of crochet through the top of the felt and into the foam.

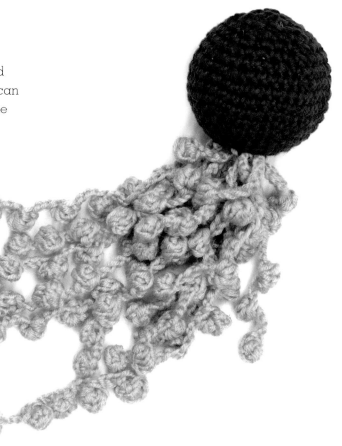

Crocheted soil

For some of the projects, such as Mexican Giant Cardon (page 26), Peruvian Apple (page 74) and Bishop's Cap (page 82), I have suggested attaching the crocheted plant to some crocheted soil. This is a great way to fill your pots to display the succulent.

Crochet a sphere using a small amount of brown DK yarn. You can adjust the amount of stuffing in your soil ball to fit your pot. Below are two patterns, one for a small pot ranging 2½–2¾in (6–7cm) in diameter and another for a medium to large pot 3¼–3½in (8–9cm) in diameter. Both of these patterns use DK-weight wool.

Soil for pots 2½–2¾in (6–7cm) in diameter

Using 3.5mm (UK9:USE/4) hook, make a magic ring.

Round 1: 1 ch, 6 dc into the centre of the ring.
Round 2: 2 dc into each st (12 sts).
Round 3: (1 dc, dc2inc) 6 times (18 sts).
Round 4: (2 dc, dc2inc) 6 times (24 sts).
Rounds 5–12: Work 8 rounds straight.
Round 13: (2 dc, dc2tog) 6 times (18 sts).
Stuff firmly with polyester stuffing.
Round 14: (1 dc, dc2tog) 6 times (12 sts).
Round 15: (Dc2tog) 6 times (6 sts).
Using a tapestry needle, weave this yarn through the last dc sts of the round and gather hole together.
Fasten off and weave in ends.

Soil for pots 3¼–3½in (8–9cm) in diameter

Using 3.5mm (UK9:USE/4) hook, make a magic ring.

Round 1: 1 ch, 6 dc into the centre of the ring.
Round 2: 2 dc into each st (12 sts).
Round 3: (1 dc, dc2inc) 6 times (18 sts).
Round 4: (2 dc, dc2inc) 6 times (24 sts).
Round 5: (3 dc, dc2inc) 6 times (30 sts).
Round 6: (4 dc, dc2inc) 6 times (36 sts).
Rounds 7–14: Work 8 rounds straight.
Round 15: (4 dc, dc2tog) 6 times (30 sts).
Round 16: (3 dc, dc2tog) 6 times (24 sts).
Round 17: (2 dc, dc2tog) 6 times (18 sts).
Stuff firmly with polyester stuffing.
Round 18: (1 dc, dc2tog) 6 times (12 sts).
Round 19: (Dc2tog) 6 times (6 sts).
Using a tapestry needle, weave this yarn through the last dc sts of the round and gather hole together.
Fasten off and weave in ends.

Crocheted pots

You can buy or recycle small plant pots that you have around the home to display your crocheted succulents. But why not crochet your own? If you crochet a pot, you can choose any colours you like. I find it useful to add some structure by covering a cardboard pot used for seedlings.

FINISHED SIZE

The pot is 2½in (6cm) in diameter at the top and 2in (5cm) in diameter at the bottom. It is 2½in (6cm) high.

YOU WILL NEED

Plain pot

◆ Stylecraft Life DK, 75% acrylic, 25% wool (326yd/298m per 100g ball): 1 ball in 2448 Bark (A)

Striped pot

◆ Rico Essentials Cotton DK, 100% cotton (142yd/130m per 50g ball): 1 ball in 90 Black (A) 1 ball in 80 White (B)

Funky pot

◆ Rico Essentials Cotton DK, 100% cotton (142yd/130m per 50g ball): 1 ball in 14 Fuchsia (A) 1 ball in 80 White (B)

All pots

◆ 3mm (UK11:US–) crochet hook
◆ 1 x biodegradable pot 2½in (6cm) in diameter
◆ Craft glue

TENSION

Tension is not essential for these projects.

> ### Note
>
> *Each pot is worked in spirals using the standard amigurumi technique.*

Plain pot

Using 3mm (UK11:US–) hook and A, make a magic ring.

Round 1: 1 ch, 8 dc into the centre of the ring.

Round 2: 2 dc into each st (16 sts).

Round 3: (1 dc, dc2inc) 8 times (24 sts).

Rounds 4–5: Work 2 rounds straight.

Round 6: Work 1 round tbl (24 sts).

Round 7: (2 dc, dc2inc) 8 times (32 sts).

Rounds 8–9: Work 2 rounds straight.

Round 10: (3 dc, dc2inc) 8 times (40 sts).

Rounds 11–12: Work 2 rounds straight.

Round 13: (4 dc, dc2inc) 8 times (48 sts).

Rounds 14–18: Work 5 rounds straight.

Rounds 19–20: Work 2 rounds tbl (48 sts).

Fasten off and weave in ends.

Striped pot

Using 3mm (UK11:US–) hook and A, make a magic ring.

Round 1: 1 ch, 8 dc into the centre of the ring.

Round 2: 2 dc into each st (16 sts).

Round 3: (1 dc, dc2inc) 8 times (24 sts).

Rounds 4–5: Work 2 rounds straight.

Round 6: Work 1 round tbl (24 sts).

Round 7: (2 dc, dc2inc) 8 times (32 sts).

Rounds 8–9: Change to B, work 2 rounds straight.

Round 10: Change to A, (3 dc, dc2inc) 8 times (40 sts).

Round 11: Work 1 round straight.

Round 12: Change to B, work 1 round straight.

Round 13: (4 dc, dc2inc) 8 times (48 sts).

Rounds 14–15: Change to A, work 2 rounds straight.

Rounds 16–17: Change to B, work 2 rounds straight.

Round 18: Change to A, work 1 round straight.

Rounds 19–20: Work 2 rounds tbl (48 sts).

Fasten off and weave in ends.

Funky pot

Using 3mm (UK11:US–) hook and A, make a magic ring.

Round 1: 1 ch, 8 dc into the centre of the ring.

Round 2: 2 dc into each st (16 sts).

Round 3: (1 dc, dc2inc) 8 times (24 sts).

Rounds 4–5: Work 2 rounds straight. In the next row and every following row, work with the two colours, leaving a strand of the colour you are not using just above your work so that it is captured by the yarn you are working.

Round 6: Place a marker at the beginning of each round, (3 dc tbl in A, 3 dc tbl in B) 4 times (24 sts).

Round 7: (3 dc in A, 3 dc in B) 4 times (24 sts).

Round 8: (2 dc, dc2inc in A, 2 dc, dc2inc in B) 4 times (32 sts).

Rounds 9–10: (4 dc in A, 4 dc in B) 4 times (32 sts).

Round 11: (3 dc, dc2inc in A, 3 dc, dc2inc in B) 4 times (40 sts).

Rounds 12–15: (5 dc in A, 5 dc in B) 4 times (40 sts).

Rounds 16–17: Fasten off yarn B and working in A only work 2 rounds straight.

Rounds 18–19: Work 2 rounds tbl (40 sts).

Fasten off and weave in ends.

Making up

Cover the outside of the cardboard pot with some craft glue. Carefully pull the crochet over the pot, making sure the top of the crocheted pot covers the cardboard. Leave to dry.

Resources

Listed here are ideas for yarn suppliers and for creative inspiration.

UK

Black Sheep Wools
Warehouse Studios
Glaziers Lane
Culcheth
Warrington
Cheshire
WA3 4AQ
www.blacksheepwools.com

Fred Aldous
Online, plus shops in Leeds,
Manchester and Sheffield
www.fredaldous.co.uk

Hobbycraft
www.hobbycraft.co.uk

John Lewis
www.johnlewis.com

Love Crochet
www.lovecrafts.com

Stylecraft
Stylecraft Yarns
Spa Mill
New Street
Slaithwaite
HD7 5BB
www.stylecraft-yarns.co.uk

USA

America's Knitting
www.americasknitting.com

Hobby Lobby
Stores nationwide
www.hobbylobby.com

Knitting Garden
www.knittinggarden.org

Michaels
Stores nationwide
www.michaels.com

Webs
www.yarn.com

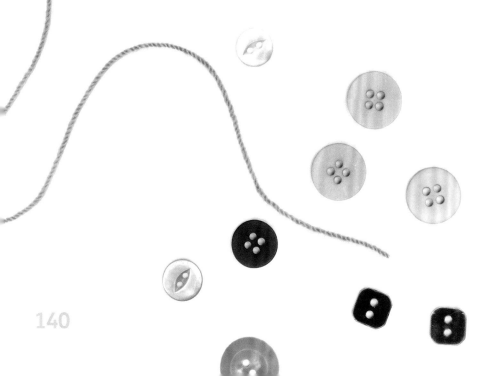

INSPIRATIONAL BOOKS

Happy Cactus: Choose it, Love it, Let it Thrive by John Pilbeam (Penguin Random House, 2018)

Prick: Cacti and Succulents: Choosing, Styling, Caring by Gynell Leon (Mitchell Beazley, 2017)

The Little Book of Cacti and Other Succulents by Emma Sibley (Quadrille Publishing, 2017)

Bring The Outside In: The Essential Guide to Cacti, Succulents, Planters and Terrariums by Val Bradley (Bantam Press, 2016)

House of Plants: Living with Succulents, Air Plants and Cacti by Rose Ray and Caro Langton (Frances Lincoln, 2016)

Botanical Style: Inspirational decorating with nature, plants and florals by Selina Lake (Ryland Peters & Small, 2016)

INSPIRATIONAL WEBSITES

I can easily lose a few hours browsing on Pinterest, the virtual moodboard site.
pinterest.com

Succulent and cactus inspiration

Surreal Succulents have a wonderful website full of inspiring plants for you to create:
surrealsucculents.co.uk

Fairy Blooms offer inspiring ideas of how to display succulents.
fairyblooms.com

Crochet inspiration

The blog of Lucy at Attic 24 is a crochet institution – a must for all those new to the craft:
attic24.typepad.com

Have a look at the lovely work of Sarah-Jane.
floanddot.blogspot.com

Most days I like to check out the inspirational tutorials of New York craft shop Purl Soho:
purlsoho.com/create

Acknowledgements

We began to laugh so much when we talked about this book. Much of the enjoyment of creating these patterns has been shared with the wonderful team at GMC. They have a passion and dedication to ensure that your craft books are the very best, and I am fortunate to work with them.

My editor Wendy is invaluable: she makes me smile, and I am inspired to do better because of her faith in me. Thank you also to Jonathan Bailey, the publisher, who trusts me to come up with appealing projects. Thanks must also go to the wonderful photographer, Neal Grundy, the illustrator Martin Woodward and to Wayne Blades for the overall design. Thank you also to Jude Roust and Nicola Hodgson who did a wonderful job checking everything.

I would also like to thank a number of yarn producers and retailers for their support. Thanks to Stylecraft Ltd and the team at Spa Mill, Annabelle, Juliet, Sophie and Anna, who generously donated many of the yarns for these projects. Thanks to Sara and the team at Black Sheep Wools for their ongoing support and for being a fab yarn shop – I was so inspired by the tinsel and eyelash yarn that they stock.

Thank you to Brenda at Bud Garden Centre for providing lots of the quirky pots and who encouraged Benjamin in his love of plants.

A quick thank you to my Birthday Ladies – Katie, Charls, Hannah, Lucy, Jo, Gemma and Lucy – we keep each other straight.

Thanks to Lucy (Attic 24) and Christine (Winwick Mum) for being my crafty best friends, putting up with my madness, and cheerleading me on. You are a joy to my heart.

I am grateful that my family joins me in laughter and excitement at the mad things I create. Benjamin and Robert, I love you.

Index

To place an order, contact:

GMC Publications Ltd
Castle Place, 166 High Street,
Lewes, East Sussex,
BN7 1XU
United Kingdom
Tel: +44 (0)1273 488005
www.gmcbooks.com